T0193458

G*It's*OD

Autum Augusta

Order this book online at www.trafford.com
or email orders@trafford.com

Most Trafford titles are also available at major online book retailers.

Print information available on the last page.

ISBN: 978-1-6987-1539-1 (sc)
ISBN: 978-1-6987-1540-7 (hc)
ISBN: 978-1-6987-1541-4 (e)

Library of Congress Control Number: 2023946978

Trafford rev. 09/20/2023

www.trafford.com
North America & international
toll-free: 844-688-6899 (USA & Canada)
fax: 812 355 4082

Contents

It Is All God.

From great miracles to funny stories, God wants us to enjoy life, laugh, and encourage the world around us for Him.

Testimonies

I had just received word that my eighty-one-year-old cousin Ted had just gone home to be with the Lord. His father had died of heart problems when Ted was six months old, one sister was two, and his other sister was three. Their mother was having a hard time financially.

My aunt had a high-school education and was hired to teach in a one-room school because a certified teacher could not be found. The state gave my aunt permission to start Ted in first grade—one year early.

Ted was about three when he became very ill. It looked like he was going to die. My aunt saved enough money to travel to Oklahoma to an Oral Roberts meeting. Oral prayed over Ted, and Ted came home healed. He lived almost seventy-eight more years.

What Do You Want?

Mrs. Brown was a teacher in the local school. She was concerned about the way drugs were coming into the school. She set up a date for Christian services with three young men who were going to a college in Oklahoma. They were preparing to become ministers. She advertised across their small town and ended up knowing all the young people who came to the meetings.

One of the "ministers" had his hair in an Afro and wore striped overalls. He saw a group of students sitting in the park, passing their bongs around. He made a short run to jump over their bonfire, shouting, "You are all going to hell if you don't change your ways!"

The students were so scared they ran into the building and into the meeting. That night, twenty-two young people made Jesus their Savior. One of them was what the town called the town junkie, Fritz. The next Monday, after school, Fritz came by Mrs. Brown's place.

Fritz was not very clean, but Mrs. Brown invited him in. "Fritz, I am so glad to see you again. How are you doing since Saturday night?"

Fritz came into the kitchen and jumped up on the counter. "I became a Christian Saturday night. And now what?" he asked.

"You can come by here every evening after school if you want," Mrs. Brown replied.

When Mrs. Brown taught Fritz two years earlier, she thought he was mentally challenged, but she discovered he was very bright. He even told her what was in her medicine cabinet and what it would do. She did not know that at that time, he was going to some friends' houses and getting high every day at noon. When he needed a fix, Mrs. Brown would read scripture to him and pray.

Part 2

"Aunt Jeanie, my mother has been sick in bed for several months. I was wondering if you could drive into another state to pray for her healing," niece LaDon said.

"It is only three hours away. I think I can do that," Jeanie said. "And I can take Fritz with me, so I won't have to travel alone."

The next weekend, Jeanie and Fritz traveled to the place where LaDon's family lived. They walked into a very dirty house and saw a lady lying in a very dirty bed. "We have come to take you to a healing meeting at your church and pray for your healing."

"I am so glad, but I don't know if I can get out of bed or not. I fell and broke my arm two weeks ago. It is in a cast," Betty explained.

It took a lot of work to get Betty to church, but with Fritz's help, they finally made it. The speaker brought a message on healing. Everyone lined up for him to touch them and be prayed over individually. Betty screamed, "I feel great, and look at my arm. It is healed too!" She took off the cast and started swinging it around and bending it.

Everyone was excited and happy. Jeanie and Fritz went home the next day. They heard two weeks later that Betty crawled back into the dirty bed and died a few weeks later. "She had been sick so long that she didn't know how to live well," someone said.

Jesus asked many people what they wanted before He healed them. Not everyone wants to be healed.

A Christmas Testimony

Hope—an interesting word. We don't realize how we live with hope daily and how much of our future is tied up with hope. It's when hope fails or, even more so, when we have no hope that life takes on a totally different outlook. There I was some thirty years ago. No hope, just on a merry-go-round going nowhere—just round and round.

I was tired of life—bored with life. Being a wife and mother of six children, I saw no future, just endless, meaningless daily chores. Emptiness. No meaning, no purpose, no hope.

Suicide! That seemed to be the answer to a tired, disillusioned thirty-four-year-old mother. The children were beautiful, and I had a wonderful husband. But what about me? I felt empty inside. Having searched through many avenues—education, witchcraft, and a host of other things—I still found the same old emptiness. Life seemed to me like a giant jigsaw puzzle but with one—only one—piece missing. There had to be one piece that put it all together. Deep down, I knew that secret lay in the one missing piece. But what was that piece?

In October 1970, I began to have those nagging feelings of depression and hopelessness, which I experienced the fall before. I hate fall. Everything dying. Everything looked dismal and lifeless. I was trapped in thoughts of just wanting to end it all.

Suicide! That was the only way I could see to end my meaningless existence. So I spent a lot of time thinking of the best way. But then, I would think about my children. Who would love them the way I did?

Sometime in late November, my nerves were shot, and I just thought that I couldn't take this anymore. I asked my husband to take the children and go somewhere—anywhere. I just needed to be alone.

As he left with all the children, I ran into the bedroom, shut the door, threw myself on the bed, and cried out, "God, if you're there, help me!" No voices, no anything—or so I thought—but a nighty hand was guiding me, one that I couldn't see or feel.

Thanksgiving came and went. My spirit lifted as I looked toward Christmas. I began to feel alive again. Christmas! A time of excitement and fun! My family had always made such a fuss over Christmas when I was growing up. Not the Christ of Christmas but one of gifts, shopping, parties, and fun. The tree, the lights, the razzle-dazzle, which comes only at the special time of year.

How well I do remember that Christmas, one I can never forget! It was Christmas 1970. A special year as astronomers were looking for a phenomenal lineup of stars to produce a brilliant huge star-like effect. They believed it could have been the same phenomenon that shone over Bethlehem almost two thousand years before.

Our children were snuggled in their beds with visions of Santa Claus putting gifts in their heads. Mr. Santa had put cookies and milk out for good old Saint Nick. (Then he went to bed.) There was such a feeling of peace in our quiet little house.

I was drawn to our bedroom window, which opened to the south. I just had to see this phenomenal star! As I looked out our window that early Christmas morning, I saw *the star*. It was so huge, so brilliant!

As I gazed at it, the most amazing thing happened: the love of God showered over me. I was transformed then and there. Peace like I had never known flooded my soul. I had been born again by God's transforming power. It was so real I wanted to get up on the roof and shout to the whole town, "World, God loves you!" It has been almost forty years since that night. I had found the missing piece to the puzzle of life: *Jesus*! What an honor to be born again on Christmas Day!

May you find Him as Lord, Savior, redeemer, and friend as I have.

The Twenty-Dollar Bill

—•——✠——•—

My husband and I had taken the youth group of seventeen kids up for a few days at Jim's Cabin, high in the Rocky Mountains above Salida, Colorado.

On a particular day, we did the arduous climb up to Boss Lake. That afternoon, after a light lunch, we headed for home and loaded on the flatbed International truck.

Finally, there was the dreaded task of cleaning the cabin. Rock floor swept, carpet sweeper ran on the rug, kitchen counters and stove cleaned, floors swept and mopped, and then the final shutting of the blinds and drawing of curtains. Cabin in shape, yard in order, we climbed the hill and loaded gear and bodies into the truck. Our plans were to stop and cook supper on our way down to the Arkansas River Canyon.

Little did we know it would be raining, so there were no fires. But God knows everything long before we do. On the hike down from Boss Lake, all the young people jostled, running and chattering all the way. My husband and I brought up the rear, assuring no one was left behind.

My husband spotted something caught in a bush: a twenty-dollar bill. All the kids had run past the bush and, in their haste, never saw it. We stopped in Canon City and were able to buy nineteen one-dollar hamburgers. Total cost—nineteen dollars plus tax.

By the way, my husband and I had no money. If one of the happy kids had found it, although everyone had passed by the same bush on the narrow path, I'm fairly sure they might have just pocketed it, not saying a word. God saw to it that we had a good meal, and no one would know that we did not have money to feed the hungry teenagers.

I Love You, Daddy

It was getting later and later. We had planned to go out to see my mother and daddy that Sunday afternoon. We had planned to go at 4:00 p.m., but there had been an unending stream of company.

Now, it was eight thirty. Everyone but my husband and our six kids were left. I said, "Okay, let's go on out to the folks."

He said, "No, it's getting too late."

I couldn't persuade him, so I announced that I was going anyway. Even though Daddy had been through seventy-nine radiation treatments for cancer, he went up early every morning and dressed and combed his hair in the usual manner.

The folks and I went to the kitchen, and Dad sat at the table across from me. I commented on how good he looked. Mother got her favorite Easter treat, a Brach's cream-filled Easter egg, and gave it to us to share. It reminded me of a sweet communion between Daddy and me as we shared it.

Daddy looked so good! Maybe the treatments were working! After visiting, I got up to leave, and Daddy sat down in his favorite recliner.

As I went to leave and had my hand on the doorknob, the Lord spoke to my heart, "Go back and giver your dad a hug." We were not a hugging family. Mother, being of English and Scottish descent, was very stoic. We knew Daddy loved us kids, but he never showed it. As I bent down to hug Daddy, the Lord instructed again, "Tell him that you love him."

"I love you, Daddy," I said as I hugged him.

Then I was gone. Little did I know that in five hours, he would be in heaven. What a special time God gave me. And I am glad I did what God told me to do.

The Rice Story

━━━━ ⚔ ━━━━

Food was scarce, and money was tight in those early days of ministry. My husband had quit his good-paying job with the Santa Fe Railroad to go into a full-time ministry. All we had that night was a small pan of cooked rice for supper to feed the eight of us.

My husband and I had privately talked earlier that we would not say anything to the kids, and we would eat as if there was enough for all of us. I placed the lid on the small amount of cooked rice. As we prayed and thanked God for the food, I just knew the rice would be multiplied.

As I removed the lid, I was disappointed. There was no more rice than when I had placed the lid on the pan. As I began to spoon out the rice into the kids' plates, I just kept spooning and spooning and spooning.

There was plenty of rice for all of us. Our tummies were full. It reminded me of the Bible story of the fishes and loaves. We didn't have five thousand people, but we were taken care of. God provides and provides abundantly.

Empty Your Purse

We had been on a family trip to my husband's sister on a farm about ten miles out of the tiny town of Genoa, Colorado. They were having a big revival meeting at the La Junta football stadium. God spoke to me on the way home to empty my purse when the offering bucket was passed. I knew I didn't have much, but I wanted to be obedient.

Our family sat down in the bleachers. One of our youths, Titus, was sitting beside me. As they were passing the big Kentucky Fried Chicken bucket, I started digging in my purse. No bills, just change. God said again, "Empty it," so I did down to the last penny. There was less than a dollar in change.

When I took out the last coin, Titus put a twenty-dollar bill in my open billfold to give. Amazing God! God honors obedience.

Pizza and Pepsi

Joe was one of the many youths we worked with in the coffeehouse days. He had been born in Mexico; but he, his mother, and siblings moved to the United States when he was six years old. He could speak English and was a good student when he attended our Christian school. Our administrator and helper had gone to training in Dallas, Texas, and left me to run the school while they were gone.

One day, Joe walked into the school office and announced that he was quitting school. Shocked and disappointed, I asked him why. He informed me that he was tired of putting up his flag and waiting on some teacher to see what he needed. He announced he was joining the marines. He followed through with that decision.

Some weeks later, he told us he had orders to report to California for basic training. Since he was leaving in a few days, my husband and I asked him to have lunch with us. He readily agreed.

My husband and I were used to God providing our needs, and we never thought about having money, which we didn't. We just didn't concern ourselves with the issue. A day or two before our appointed lunch date, we asked Joe where he would like to eat. We were surprised when he happily said, "Pizza Hut."

My husband and I thought that was kind of a pricey place, but hiding our surprise, we said, "Sure." Thinking that Joe might be more comfortable, we invited out son, Kris, to go with us. We were still not concerned with the financial part. In those days, there were no "lunch buffet" specials. But God is tremendous!

At about nine in the morning, we got a call from Pizza Hut. No reservations of any kind had been made. We also did not discuss our plans with anyone. The voice on the phone said, "Dr. Messersmith, our local dentist, has paid for a meal for four and can't make it. Would you be interested in coming in for the meal?" This included pizza of choice, salad bar, and drinks. We barely knew Dr. Messersmith.

It was a hot day, and we quickly downed the pitcher of iced Pepsi as we enjoyed our meal. My husband and I knew we didn't even have enough money even for the Pepsi. I quickly closed my eyes and said a quick prayer of thank you. By that time, we were out of Pepsi, and I watched a family leave their table, leaving a pitcher almost full of Pepsi.

Our son, Kris, was embarrassed when his father walked over to the table and took the pitcher of Pepsi. Our God is a God of abundant supply.

Jesus Is the Giver of Life

Living in a highly populated Hispanic area was a group of eight students, including my husband and us, who wanted to know more Spanish than the little they knew. Our daughter-in-law, Sandy, took the challenge to teach us.

Nights were fun as we met weekly and gathered around our desk, which was really a ping-pong table in the basement of our home. Classes were fun but challenging. Assignments took time while we studied during the week, learning to conjugate the verbs and all their tenses.

After some months, the session was over. We decided to celebrate and go to El Azteca. While we were eating in a café, Jean, the matriarch of the Munoz family and co-owner and co-operator, approached us.

Her face was somber as she walked over to our table, preciously carrying a small bundle wrapped in a baby blanket. She said, "Will you pray for my little granddaughter? The doctors have given her no hope. She is dying. A failure-to-survive baby."

The spirit of death was strong in her. I couldn't even touch her. None of us could. My husband always loved to hold newborns. He gently took her in his arms. We all joined in prayer for her. We learned some weeks later that she was thriving. In fact, in a few years, she was actually taller and healthier than her two older brothers.

Morgan became a picture of health. God is the healer!

Thousand-Dollar Faith

"Something has got to be done" was echoing in my mind. We had been hauling water for our house and livestock for several years using our International truck and 1,200-gallon steel water tank. After years of use, the tank had rusted and was now leaking.

The man we bought the water from was unhappy because he said his other customers were complaining that our leaking tank was making a muddy mess for them to drive in when they filled their tanks.

My husband had a solution. He was a welder and had already patched the tank several times. That would last for a while. He finally decided to turn the tank over so the better part of the tank would not leak. That lasted for a while, but then, it started to leak again. More complaints!

As a last resort, my husband crawled inside and sealed the whole tank from the inside. After some time, the tank started to leak again. We needed our own water supply but certainly didn't have the money for a well that we someday wanted to drill. I discouragingly sat down in a chair to cry out to the Lord. I said, "Lord, we need ten-thousand-dollar faith, and I only have one-thousand-dollar faith." Sometimes God "adds," and sometimes He "multiplies."

I received a phone call early the next week. It was my sister. "Are you sitting down?"

I said, "Yes."

She said, "Can you use ten thousand dollars?"

Oh, God's provisions! Little did I know the drilling would end up being twelve thousand dollars. Then there was the casing to pay for, along with a huge compressor to pump air into the well for the airlift system we needed.

A few weeks later, there was another ten thousand dollars from my mother and father's estate. That paid for everything needed for the well and the whole water system!

My God shall supply all your needs according to *HIS* riches in glory (Philippians 4:19l).

Fill 'Er Up

$$\bullet\!\!-\!\!\bullet\ \ \rightleftharpoons\!\!\diamond\!\!\rightleftharpoons\ \ \bullet\!\!-\!\!\bullet$$

It was a lovely early summer day. Our little family had loaded up, heading home after going to church that Sunday morning. After fixing a quick lunch, I headed back to the station wagon. I was looking forward to helping at the jail service and being a part of the preaching and testifying of the things God was doing. What a blessing to share Jesus with the prisoners.

As I started down the street, I glanced down at the gas gage. I sighed; the gage read about a hair's breadth from empty.

"That man! Hadn't my husband even looked at the gas gage? God, we've been doing your work, and here I am, out of gas again!" Oh well, it was only a couple of miles from our house to the jail. I was in a hurry to make the 1:00 p.m. jail service. I would figure out the gas problem after the service!

Since this was a volunteer program, we were never sure who would show up to help. To my surprise, a young lady named Jennifer was there. Jennifer had been one of our original young people. I had not seen her for over two-plus years. We have had no connection of any kind.

At that time, I had confronted her over some questionable moral conduct she had displayed.

We had taken her on a bus trip with a youth group to a conference in Indiana. I had told her sharply, "I don't care what you do when you get back home, but you won't pull that junk while you are traveling with us!"

After that trip, we had no contact with her. Now, here she was, volunteering at the jail service. I told her I would give her a ride home, hoping to renew a very estranged relationship. Not thinking, I offered her a ride home to Rocky Ford, about twelve miles away.

We had been living by faith for several years. You honestly don't think about money. I had an itsy-bitsy amount of gas *and* no money for gas. My focus was on doing God's work that day, the jail service.

Jennifer and I climbed into the station wagon. I started it and just began to drive. What else could I do? I told her that I would take her home!

As we were on our way, going down the highway and heading for Rocky Ford, the needle on the gas gage began to climb up, up, and up! I watched it move up to almost half of a tank full. Thank you, Jesus! Oh, and Jennifer? She is a strong Christian to this day!

$9+1=10$

—•— ⚔ —•—

It was eleven thirty in the morning, and I was busy doing paperwork in the little front office at our Bridge over Troubled Waters Coffeehouse. Our full-time live-in helper, Anna Mae, interrupted my progress and asked, "What shall I fix for dinner?"

I responded with a quick "What's in there?"

Her reply was "There isn't anything."

"Well, just make tortillas then."

She explained, "There isn't anything. No, nothing."

"Well, I will figure it out. I want to get this paperwork done by noon. Then, we'll see," I said.

At exactly noon, one of our youths, Angel, came through the door bearing gifts: ten delicious A&W ultimate hamburgers! Angel delivered newspapers for the local *Tribune-Democrat*, and they had treated their paper boys to the A&W hamburgers. There were nine of us living at the coffeehouse: LaVern and me, our six children, and one helper.

About fifteen minutes later, a hobo who had been "riding the rails" came up our sidewalk. We asked him if he had had lunch. He said no. After giving thanks to God, we enjoyed this timely provision.

God's ways are so perfect! 2 + 6 + 1 + 1 = 10! Wow!

Polly's Healing from Allergies

———— ✦ ————

We first discovered my daughter's allergies when she was only two weeks old. She would have spells of diarrhea and vomiting. A well-meaning but know-it-all nurse friend decided she was allergic to me, her mother's milk. So, we put her on canned baby formula. She would still have the same reaction.

After we had seen the family doctor, he put her on a soy-based formula. This helped some. It was also discovered she could not have anything with sugar. Even though my mother, who lived next door, insisted she could have graham crackers. That would make her sick wish the same symptoms.

The doctor suggested that we would just observe what made her react in the usual manner. We began to watch and eliminate those foods. So no dairy products and nothing with sugar. We began to eliminate any fruit from her diet one by one. Finally, all fruits of any kind. The same thing with any vegetables. The only thing she could tolerate was potatoes. (That is if you consider a potato a vegetable.) As far as meat, there was not much she could eat.

She virtually lived on canned shrimp, potatoes, and special soybean milk. As Polly was nearing her second birthday, we knew we had to do something! She was content with her bottle of the soy-based formula. It had a horrible smell and, I'm sure, a bad taste also. When we weaned her, I knew she would never take it in a cup. What were we to do? Even though we weren't big on medicine or medical doctors, as a last resort, we made an appointment with our family physician to get a referral to an allergy specialist in Pueblo.

Finally, arrangements were made. The date was set to go to Pueblo. While we waited for the appointment, a strange thing happened.

The specialist, instead of hiring a professional, decided he would save money and trim his own trees. Not a good idea. He fell from the tree, broke several bones, and ended up in the hospital. Now what?

Our friend and mentor, a strong Christian brother James Brown, agreed to come and pray for Polly's healing. They prayed a prayer of faith and then headed back home to Rocky Ford. I would like to say that the next day, my faith was strong. It wasn't. Although Polly watched her five older siblings eat all kinds of food and sugary things. She never asked (or cried) for any of it. That in itself was pretty amazing. Now, the next day after she had been prayed for, she wanted ice cream, asking many times that day. Ice cream was the worst thing she could have asked for. Sugar and milk.

I gave God all day to heal her! It wasn't only ice cream she wanted; it was all kinds of things she was allergic to. At four o'clock, I thought maybe God had had enough time to heal her. So I pulled out the ice cream and gave her a bowl. Nothing!

In the days that followed, she ate whatever the rest of us was eating. God truly healed her! Isaiah 53 and 2 Peter 2:24 tell us that by His stripes (blood shed by the whips laid on Jesus's back), *we are healed*. Thank you, Jesus!

Joey's Healing

After a long twenty-two-hour labor, my second son was born, a nice, healthy eight-pound-and-four-ounce baby. Joey was the fifth child with three older sisters. Within two weeks, I began to notice a breathing problem. He was the only one of our children who was allowed to sleep in our bedroom. It was a rather scary time. Wondering if he would just stop breathing, I took him to the doctor more than once, concerned about a bad cold. The doctor thought little about it.

When Joey was several months old, our neighbor Louise, who lived across the street from us, came to visit. She heard Joey's breathing and said, "He has asthma."

The doctor raised his voice and yelled, "I am the doctor here!" It would be his opinion, not ours! Someone suggested that we should use an antihistamine. We bought some and gave him one dose. We all know that one dose of it does not cure anyone! This was God's first miracle in Joey's life. Yes, we used it only *one* time. Never again did he have any more breathing problems—no, not one more time.

Joey did have one other problem: an allergy to chocolate. This really was frustrating to a student in early elementary school. The chocolate-milk day was every Thursday. Seemed like every mother who was coming to school for their child's birthday brought cholate cupcakes loaded with chocolate frosting. His reaction to chocolate was just like his sister's: vomiting and diarrhea.

About a week after his sister Polly's healing, we had friends over one evening. Joey had seen his sister's healing. He shyly asked for prayer for his allergy. We prayed, and almost immediately, he asked if we would go to a 7-Eleven and buy chocolate milk. Oh, the faith of a child.

Joey had chocolate milk that night, and for a year, he ate and drank to his heart's desire. That was almost fifty years ago, and he has had no problems since.

Waiting for Eight Years

John Harbert Campo

In 1942, a dump truck fell on my head and neck, breaking my collarbone and tearing my shoulder blade loose, also injuring my spine. Two years later, a cow threw me on my head, breaking a bone at the base of my neck and wrecking my nerves. It later caused me to have arthritis of the spine.

At that time, my whole right side would apparently go to sleep; and once it was completely paralyzed and I was prayed for, God touched me, bringing the feeling back. I would have severe pain at the base of my head, between my shoulders, and all down my spine. During this time, I went to a lot of doctors. I would visit one place after another, following people's advice on things that might help me. Despite my efforts, none of it seemed to make much of a difference for me. My whole right side was smaller than the left.

I was prayed over many times, and God would touch me, but I never got completely healed.

I went about three years ago to Dr. C. Robert Stark at 1459 Ogden Street, Denver, Colorado, who was a bone specialist. He had me wear a brace on my head and neck for four months, and when I quit wearing it, the other doctors said it did me more harm than good. I also went to Halstead, Kansas, and went through the clinic there. I took their medicine, but I was still no better.

I went to six doctors in my hometown. I also went to one in Trinidad, Colorado; one in Pueblo, Colorado; one in Pampa, Texas; another one in Denver, Colorado; and another in Amarillo, Texas. They said there was absolutely no cure for me and would not take my case. The last doctor I went to before I was healed was in Boise City, Oklahoma. I doctored there for quite a while, and he gave me a number of shots and thought they would get me on my feet to where I would be able to go to Oklahoma City for an operation.

I had been walking on crutches most of the time then since December 1949. I hardly did any work or provided for my family of a wife and five children.

I went to Amarillo, Texas, on September 1, 1950, where Rev. Oral Roberts was holding a tent-healing campaign.

I was prayed for on September 5, and God wonderfully healed me. I walked down the aisle without my crutches, put them in my pickup, and drove 150 miles home without pain, which I hadn't been free from for years. I felt like a new man.

Praise the good Lord. I am now preaching the gospel.

You may use my testimony as it may be a help to someone close to turn their faith loose and trust in God.

The Physical Benefit of Praying or Speaking in Tongues

━━━━◆━━━━

God had made provision for you and me to be whole, to be well, and to have access to his healing process. There is a study that has been done by Dr. Carl Peterson. This study revealed that there is an available for our own benefit. Dr. Carl Peterson worked on this study at ORU in Tulsa, Oklahoma, a few years ago. Being a brain specialist, he was doing research on the relationship between the brain and praying or speaking in tongues. Some amazing things were discovered.

Through research and testing, he found out that as we pray in the Spirit or worship in the Spirit (our heavenly language), there is an activity that begins to take place in our brain. As we engage in our heavenly language, the brain releases two chemicals that are directed into our immune system. This promotes healing within our bodies. Amazingly, these secretions are triggered from a part of the brain that has no other apparent activity in humans. It is only activated by our Spirit-led prayer and worship.

Before the fall of man, did God, in his perfect creation, provide for the total healing of mankind in this manner? As Adam walked and communicated with the Father in the garden, was this close and intimate fellowship and communication causing divine health to flow in his body? Just something for us to think about.

God is the restorer of all things. As we exercise our life in the Spirit by speaking in the heavenly language that He has put within us, we are touching the supernatural power of God, and we are letting Him restore a part of what was lost.

Now science has proved the process, and you and I can turn this healing process on through our relationship with our Heavenly Father. Just one more great reason to be filled with the Holy Spirit and commune with the Father in your heavenly language.

According to the Holy Spirit speaking through the apostle Paul, "He who speaks in a tongue edifies himself (1 Corinthians 14:4). We always thought of the edification as only spiritual edification, which is great and always needed, but Christian psychiatrist Carl R. Peterson, MD, describes physical edification also! Isn't God amazing?

We have found on the internet documentation from Dr. Peterson's office that he is a highly respected psychiatrist and a Christian.

Note: Dr. Peterson begins his attachment by specifically referring to praying in the Spirit (speaking in tongues) and then begins to just use the words prayer of praying. Throughout his paper, he refers to speaking in tongues. It is the context of the whole paper and is introduced by his letter.

CHRISTIAN-PSYCHIATRY SERVICES, INC.

Dear friend,

Thank you for your inquiry regarding the relationship of extended periods of praying in tongues and joyful laughter to brain activity. As you will read in the enclosed explanation, I shared some information concerning this with several ministers at a gathering some time ago. I pray this information will be helpful to you.

EFFECTS OF EXTENDED VERBAL PRAYER AND JOYFUL LAUGHTER

I have a number of inquiries is concerning the efficacy of praying in the spirit (speaking in tongues) and its benefit to the human immune system, i.e. immunity enhanced by chemicals released from a part of the brain. I am attempting to clarity some information I have shared with a number of ministers. This is the information I have that may be deducted from what we know about the say the brain functions. We know the part of the brain affected most noticeably by extended prayer and laughter represents a significant portion of the brain and its metabolic activity. Therefore voluntary speech during extended vocal prayer causes a major stimulation in these parts of the brain (Mainly the hypothalamus).

The hypothalamus has direct regulation of four major systems of the body, mainly

A (the pituitary gland and all target endocrine glands.

B (the total immune system;

C (the entire autonomic system; and

D (the production of brain hormones called endorphins and enkephalins which are chemicals the body produces and are 100–200 times more powerful than morphine.

In summary, a very significant percentage of the central nervous system is directly and indirectly activated in the process of extended verbal musical prayer over a period of time. This results in a significant release of brain hormones which in turn, increases the body's general immunity. It is further enhanced through joyful laughter with increased respirations and oxygen intake to the brain, diaphragm and other muscles. This same phenomenon is seen in physical activity in general.

We know from the Word of God that there is a true joy that builds and sustains. Nehemiah tells us the joy of the Lord is our strength. There is joy in the presence of Jehovah. We as believers having entered into that wonderful presence, of our Lord, know this is to be true. What we just continue to remember is that the joy of the Lord spoken of in the Word is so much more than any manifestation. We can truly have that unspeakable joy in the face of any trials we may encounter, if our joy is grounded in a knowledge of the Lord Jesus Christ.

I hope the above information helps to clarify the report you received regarding my statement in the area of the physical effects of speaking in tongues and joyful laughter for extended periods of time. Truly, we all benefit—body, soul, and spirit—from obedience and yielding to the Spirit of God in every area of our lives.

Carl R. Peterson, MD

Kids Are Funny

Water-Log Ride

A five-year-old and I had just finished taking a water-log ride at an amusement park. When I asked her if she had gotten wet, she smiled and said, "Yes, I did, but I held it as long as I could!"

Bible: When the waters sweep over you, it will not hurt you.

Cockeyed Eating

I tried some Southern cooking one day,

And wondered if my sons would like it and say,

My eight-year-old answered my question with ease,

When he handed back his empty plate, "Mom, give me some more of those cockeyed peas [black-eyed peas]!"

He still loved to eat and said, "Mom, I don't think I want to come to your house anymore."

"Why not?" I asked.

"I eat too much. It's bad when you can't bend over and touch your toes, but it's worse when you can't even see your toes."

Bible: Taste and see that the Lord is good.

Don't Stand Still

We were moving. My husband and helpers dropped the washer.

I told the men not to worry. I would paint a picture of the dent to cover it.

I painted a sunset and was pleased and sang a song.

My son saw the painting and said,

"You better not stand still around here very long,

Or you'll have a painting on your back or your head."

Bible: The creation declares the glory of God.

Help, I'm Hungry

I caught my five-year-old in the cookie jar, and he had been misbehaving.

I sent him to bed early without any more eating.

Later, I thought I heard someone shouting outside.

I went to check it out, and what I found shook my pride.

My son was leaning out the window next to the street,

Yelling, "Someone, help me. I am locked up, and I can't get out, and I need something to eat."

Bible: Give us this day our daily bread.

"No! It's too close to dinner time for cookies," I told Ron and Bruce.

It was a week later before I heard the bad news.

The boys went to every house on our street, asking for something to eat.

"Our mothers won't feed us anymore," they said.

The neighbors fed the poor boys with whatever they had.

If there had been child abuse laws then, we would have looked very bad.

Bible: Our God shall supply all our needs in Christ Jesus.

Give Me Another One

"I have a surprise for you," said Uncle Fudd to three-year-old Charlie.

He opened his coat, and there to see was a baby cottontail bunny.

When the grandmother checked on the child and bunny minutes later,

Charlie was picking up after the bunny, saying,

"Rabbit, give me another marble, another marble, please."

Bible: The angels will bear us up on their hands lest we dash our feet against a stone.

Half of a Doctor

Willie was ten months old when he was toddling across the floor.

He fell and burned his leg on the furnace by the door.

It was a bad thing because the town did not have a doctor.

That night, when big brother said his prayers before he went to bed, he thanked God for their local pharmacist before he covered his head,

Saying, "Thank you, God, for sending half a doctor to help my little brother."

Bible: All good things come from God.

The Hell Out Of It

Six-year-old Timmy took a bite out of an apple and said,

"I sure bit the hell out of that, didn't I, Mom?"

Mother sat Timmy down and said, "Look at this apple,

There is no hell in it, see?"

And Timmy agreed.

It was time in the church for the children to break their banks of clay,

To give to missions what they had saved.

"I broke the hell out of that, didn't I?" Timmy again did say.

All the children said the same as they broke their banks of clay.

The adults were embarrassed but could not stop talking,

So beware, adults, of what you say when little ears are listening.

Children seemed to know more than the adults were guessing.

Bible: Out of the mouth of babes shall come knowledge.

What an Awful Sandwich

Two little boys were spending the night with some friends so their parents could have a date without interruption.

42

The friends decided to take the boys out for dinner and ordered them each a nice hamburger, not knowing they were just used to the meat patties.

"This is the dumbest hamburger I ever saw. It even has bread on it!" the four-year-old said.

Bible: Jesus is the bread of life.

If I Had a Hammer

It was a hot summer day. Bob (twelve) and Bill (ten) had worked all morning building a birdhouse. Bob accidentally hit Bill with his hammer.

Bill was surprised and angry, so he hit Bob with his hammer.

Bob was getting ready to hit Bill again when Bill's mother ran out of the house to keep the boys from killing each other.

The boys were still angry and promised they would hate each other forever. An hour later, they were friends again and playing together.

"You're friends again?" asked Bob's mother.

"Why do you ask?" the boys said with wonder.

Wouldn't it be nice if the whole world could bury the hammer?

Bible: We have to forgive to be forgiven.

Dangerous Exploring

It was a Christmas vacation from school. My family decided to go to the mountains to visit my sister. Her husband was in the army and stationed in Alaska, and she was living alone close to her husband's parents.

We ran into icy roads at the foot of the mountains and decided to take another less-used road and go over a pass that wasn't as high. We inched our way to the summit and could not go any farther because another car had slid sideways. It was blocking the road and was close to a hundred-foot drop-off.

As we came closer, we realized it was my other sister and her family. "If they are going to slide off the mountain, why do we have to be here to watch it?" I asked myself. I prayed for everyone's safety.

The whole family got out and pushed my sister's car back into their lane of traffic. It was scary looking down at the deep drop-off. By working together and pushing the cars over the summit, we finally conquered the pass. As we drove down the mountain, it stopped snowing, and the weather was warm again.

When we drove into my sister's driveway, everyone was glad to see us, and we were very glad to be there. We were standing outside talking when my two boys decided to go on inside my sister's new trailer home.

My youngest son unhooked what looked like a ballpoint pen that had been hanging on the kitchen wall. "What is this?" he asked his older brother.

Big brother said, "Let me have it, and I'll find out!" He took the "pen" and pulled up the shirt clip on it.

Both boys came out of the house running, screaming, and rubbing their eyes. It was a tear-gas gun. The gas was so strong we couldn't enter the house until late evening.

Only my boys could walk into a house and "shoot an ink pen." It took them exactly five minutes to do it.

Bible: Wait for the Lord, and He will direct your paths.

To and from School

It was a cold, windy day. Six inches of new snow had fallen. It was almost time for school to be out.

I wrapped my baby in a blanket and rushed to the car. I drove slowly through the falling snow to the east end of the schoolhouse to pick up my first grader. I waited a few minutes and then went inside to his room. The teacher told me he had started walking home a little early. This did not surprise me because my son loved the snow and the great outdoors.

We returned home and began to wait. After an hour of waiting, I became worried. I wrapped up my baby again and ran through the snow to the car. I drove around our little town. I couldn't find my older son. I finally went back to the house and started to call people I knew who lived between us and the school, starting with the people who lived closest to the school.

"Yes, he was here a little while ago and was carrying a lot of books. He sat down and visited for a while before he left," each person said.

I was ready to call the police when I heard him walking up the driveway. He was singing. He bounced through the door with one book in his hands.

"Where have you been, and where are the rest of your books?" I shouted. "Don't you know you are supposed to come straight home after school?"

He smiled at me and said, "I just wanted to see some of my friends. I guess I dropped the rest of my books between their houses," he answered.

I put my baby in the car for the third time, along with my older son, and we went looking for books. Have you ever gone looking for library books in deep snow and mud and after dark?

We looked for books for two hours. We found a few of them. Some of them had been run over by cars, and some of them had never been found. We ended up paying for most of the books.

Since then, the librarian has made a rule that only two books can be checked out at one time by each student.

Because he was still enjoying the great outdoors, the next spring, my son walked to school and showed up two hours late. His teacher told me that she tried to scold him, but he smiled and placed a rock collection on her desk. "I found these just for you," he said.

She did not know whether to say thank you or tell him to stay in at recess.

Bible: The gifts of the Lord are without repentance.

Flecka, My Friend

My son Ronny decided, at the age of five, that he wanted to be a cowboy. He did not have a horse, so he gave himself imaginary ones. In his imaginary world, he spent many days riding and feeding his horses. He called his favorite horse Flecka. Ronny played with Flecka for the next seven years.

It was time for the fall parent-teacher conferences. I went to school to visit my son's sixth-grade teachers and receive his progress reports.

"We are so sorry that your son's horse, Flecka, died last night. We think he has done really well just to be in school today under these circumstances. He is a very brave boy," each teacher said.

Ronny was now twelve. I did not want to embarrass him by telling his teachers that Flecka was an imaginary horse. I knew Flecka had been a big part of my son's life for a long time. I never heard him mention Flecka again.

Ronny never outgrew his love for horses. At the age of seventeen, the week after his all-state football game, he moved out of our house to be on his own. The first thing he did was go into debt for five hundred dollars to buy his first real horse. Ronny practiced night and day and soon became one of the best cowboys around.

Several people told me that my son learned fast for a kid who had never ridden a horse before. Never ridden a horse before? I wonder.

Bible: Jesus is coming back riding a white hose.

On the Way to the Market

A little preschooler was staying with her aunt. As she was playing with some younger children, the aunt heard her niece say, "This little piggy went to the market. This little piggy stayed home. This little piggy had corn for dinner, and this piggy … this little piggy … ah, this little piggy went to Walmart."

Bible: Our God shall supply all our needs according to His riches in Christ Jesus.

Pretty Girl

Four-year-old Ginger was a flower girl at her cousin's wedding. She wore a beautiful white lace dress and hat like the bride's. The next morning, I told Ginger I had seen a pretty little girl at the wedding the night before. "Yes, it was me," she sighed.

Bible: Man was made in the image of God.

Betcha Can't Eat Just One

The doorbell was ringing. Alice was greeted by three Girl Scouts when she opened the door. "We have the four boxes of cookies you ordered," the oldest girl said.

"Great! Your cookies are the best!" Alice said.

"Yes, I know. I don't know how some people can live without them or just eat one box of them," the girl replied with a sigh.

Bible: Taste and see that the Lord is good.

Two Brains?

My friend and I were working at the local pregnancy center. She was teaching a Bible class to three ladies who did not speak English. I decided I could be of help to keep a five-year-old busy while his mother was in class. His mother had said, "English," then put up her hand to measure a bit. I nodded to let her know I understood.

I found it a lot of fun to work with her son. We found some paper and drew pictures with a marker. When the class was over and they caught a ride home, I suddenly realized what the five-year-old child had done:

He was watching a cartoon on his mother's phone in Spanish and talking to me in English with no accent.

Bible: Unless you become like little children, you cannot enter the kingdom of heaven.

Flying over Jordan

It was during the Desert Storm War in Iraq when my husband and I watched a television program on birds that migrate between Africa and Europe. I told my high-school students about it the next day. I was explaining that some of the bodies of water were getting wider.

Scientists were worried about the survival of the birds if they could no longer fly back to their hatching grounds. One scientist thought the birds might find a different route to get back to Africa.

One of my freshman students looked very worried. "They better not fly over Jordan because the people of Jordan are shooting down anything that flies over Jordan!" he exclaimed.

Bible: God will put His angels in charge over you.

Octopus in School?

It was almost time for the tardy bell when one of my sixth-grade students came in with a surprise. Roger had just brought a five-gallon jar containing a preserved baby octopus in formaldehyde to school.

The students spent several minutes looking at the hideous creature before going back to their seats. We live in the middle of North America, and most of the students had never seen the ocean or an octopus.

Roger carefully placed the jar on the corner of his desk. He reached for a pencil and bumped the huge jar. The jar fell to the hardwood floor and shattered into a hundred pieces. The room was soon filled with formaldehyde fumes, and everyone was getting dizzy. Many of the girls were screaming that the monster lying on the floor was "going to get them."

The first-year teacher was trying to decide what to do. She expected one of the school board members to walk in at any time. She ordered that all the windows be opened. The teacher sent some of the students to get a roll of paper towels. She sent another student to get the janitor to help clean up the mess.

After things were under control, she called the science teacher at the high school to come after the octopus and put it back into a preserving liquid.

No one from the school board came by that day. The students were soon back to their studies. Roger was proud of his donation to the school.

Five years later, he was killed in a car accident, but the little octopus can still be seen in the high-school science room today.

Bible: When things go wrong, God will make a way of escape.

Misinterpretation

Our town has a lumber yard called Everett Moore. In a Sunday school, the children were singing, "Alive, alive, my Jesus is alive forevermore."

One of the little girls was singing, "Alive, alive, my Jesus is alive at Everett Moore."

Bible: Jesus is everywhere.

Another Misinterpretation

A schoolteacher was shocked when she heard one small child reciting the Pledge of Allegiance. Instead of saying, "One nation indivisible," the boy was saying, "One naked individual." She asked him to repeat it, and she heard him clearly.

Bible: Great is the nation whose God is the Lord.

I'm Not Afraid

It was Mrs. Patton's first year of teaching. The principal had just come into the room and announced that it was time for the students to go to the nurse's office one at a time for vaccination shots. Several students began to cry, while others told Mrs. Patton that they were afraid to take shots. Some said they were sure that their mothers would not want them to have a shot.

Mrs. Patton explained to the class that it was necessary to take their shots to keep them from getting sick. She also told them it would not hurt much.

Richard stood up. "Mrs. Patton, I'll take my shot first. I'm not afraid. I'll show the class that it doesn't hurt," he said proudly.

Richard returned to the classroom a few minutes later. "See, it didn't hurt me at all," he said and fainted.

"Richard is dead. They are trying to kill all of us!" the students screamed.

The class was so frightened that Mrs. Patton had to get the principal's help to usher the kids to the nurse's office.

Richard's mother told Mrs. Patton, "All my children faint every time they get a shot or vaccinated."

Bible: God will lift us up when we fall.

Buffalo Noise

Brad, a five-year-old, was typing on the computer. Suddenly, he stopped. "I hear a buffalo," he told his tutor.

The teacher laughed and said, "You must be imagining things. There are no buffalo around here."

A few minutes later, Brad stopped again. "I do hear a buffalo!" he shouted.

The tutor started laughing. "There is your buffalo," she said, pointing to the floor. "It is my little dog snoring under your desk."

Roger Miller's song: You can't go roller skating in a buffalo herd, but you can be happy if you have a mind to.

Computer High Score

Mrs. Brown was teaching a high-school special-education class. As a reward for finishing their work, Mrs. Brown let the students do a math Pac-Man game on the computer. It was a fun way to learn.

Mrs. Brown had the same game on her computer at home. It was also her husband's favorite game. The students were soon challenging Mr. Brown for high scores.

"I'm tired of typing my name in every time I want to play this game," Mr. Brown said one evening.

"Put Rusty's name on some of your games," Mrs. Brown said. "He is a Down syndrome student and very handicapped. I would like to see his name beside a high score," she explained.

Mr. Brown used Rusty's name and had his highest score. Mrs. Brown took the disk to school the next week to challenge her students.

It was almost time for the bell to ring for the next class when Mrs. Brown noticed that a student had accumulated a high score. "Go ahead and finish your game. I will tell your next teacher that you will be a little late and why." Mrs. Brown said. The bell rang, and she notified the other teacher.

When Mrs. Brown returned to her room, the student had beaten Pac-Man. "Oh great, that is your highest score! I'm proud of you!" she exclaimed.

"Yeah, but I barely beat Rusty," he moaned. "I don't know how he got such a high score," he added.

The rest of the students knew it was not Rusty's score, but they didn't tell. They were laughing so hard that they were almost late for their next class.

Bible: Everyone is important to God.

Garth Brooks

A teacher and a mother were visiting. Ms. Carol asked Betty if she would mind if she gave her teenage son her electric guitar.

"I haven't played the guitar for several years. I think your son might enjoy learning to play it," Carol explained.

Betty started laughing.

"What is so funny?" Carol asked.

"Several people have told my six-foot-three-inch son that he looks like Garth Brooks. He has started to wear Western clothes, and last week, he bought a big black cowboy hat to wear. I guess your guitar will make the look complete," she said.

Betty went on to tell Ms. Carol a very interesting story. She was raising her two sons and one daughter alone because their father had become too dangerous for her and her children to live with.

"We had moved to the mountains to try to start a new life," Betty said. "It had been a hard winter, and we were out of groceries and wood for our fireplace. I did not think we could survive another day. We ate the last of our food and prayed before I put the children to bed.

"Before sunup, there was a knock on the door. I put on my robe and answered the door. There were two huge men with large muscles. They said they had brought us some firewood and spent an hour stacking the wood next to the house and a large pile next to the fireplace. I said thank you several times as the two men rode off on their large sled.

"Before I could get to sleep again, I heard another knock on the door. When I answered the door, there were two different men. They were as large as the first ones. I could see a large sled loaded with groceries. The two men brought in the groceries. I could not say thank you enough times as I waved goodbye.

"I told my children that I was going to go into town and find the church that had delivered the groceries and wood, so we could thank everyone. The kids went to town with me, and we talked to the minister of every church. No one had made the deliveries or seen large men with sleds. I believe it was God's angels taking care of us when we couldn't take care of ourselves," Betty said. "The wood and groceries lasted until spring, and I had found a job so I could take care of my family.

Bible: God knows our needs before we ask and sends his angels to fulfill His will and take care of His children.

Honesty Pays

It was Mrs. Smith's job to help her special-education students complete their work from other classes. Soon other students were coming into the room to work. Mrs. Smith was concerned about some of the students. They seemed to do their math lessons too quickly, but they could not explain to Mrs. Smith how they had obtained the right answers. "There has to be some answer sheet floating around," she told herself.

Mrs. Smith went to talk to the math teacher. She asked him if he would please demand that the students show their work on their answer sheets.

The math teacher refused and said, "If they have the answers, they have gotten them from you."

One student finally confessed to Mrs. Smith that he was cheating. "Please promise me you won't cheat again, and I will help you get a good grade by just learning how to do the problems," Mrs. Smith said.

The student agreed and spent some extra time working with Mrs. Smith. Several weeks later, the student came into the room laughing.

"What's so funny?" Mrs. Smith asked.

"We had a test today. I was the only person who knew how to do the problems," he explained. "I guess honesty really does pay," he said.

Bible: The Lord is where the truth is.

Where Did Everybody Go?

Summerfield was building a new elementary school. Mrs. Root went out to do playground duty. All the students were gone except for Don. Don was a six-foot sixth grader and was rather uncoordinated.

"Where are all the other students?" Mrs. Root asked.

"I don't know. I just fell down, and when I got up, all the kids were gone." Don answered. He sounded like he thought the world was coming to an end. He was relieved when he saw eighty students follow the principal out of the new school building.

The same student told Mrs. Root that he had practiced all summer and could jump two inches high.

The next summer, Don and Jack worked for the Roots on their farm. One day, the two boys were carrying some irrigation pipe from one spot to another. They picked up one long piece and decided that there was a rabbit inside. "Let's carry it on over and catch the rabbit when we lay it down," Don told Jack.

Jack looked inside. "Let's dump one end in the pond and let it slide out. It's not a rabbit. It's a skunk," he said. The skunk swam away without "perfuming" anyone. The boys were more careful after that.

Bible: God is our protector.

Total Embarrassment

Mrs. Thompson tells about an embarrassing day as a schoolteacher. Mrs. Thompson continued,

> One year I had a student who always came into class late. It interrupted the class, and I warned the student several times. One day, I saw that he was late again, so I locked the classroom door. I told the other students what I was doing. We heard knocking on the door. Then it was still. I thought the student had been punished enough and went into the hall. The large boy was walking down the hall, crying, "The teacher locked me out, and I don't know where to go!"

> A few years later, I had another student who always came to class late. I warned the student, but it didn't seem to work. I decided to lock the student out of the room as I had done several years before. I told the students what I was doing.

> We heard a knock on the door and then quietness. Suddenly, there was a loud banging on the door.

"Quiet out there!" I shouted. The banging continued, and I hollered again. When I thought the student had been punished enough, I opened the door and looked into the angry face of my superintendent. He was so angry that he had the locks on all the doors removed by lunchtime.

"I wasn't very popular with the other teachers that day either," Mrs. Thompson said.

Bible: God does not want any to perish, so the gate to heaven is open to all who believe.

Where?

One five-year-old told me that she had a freckle on her "China." I'll let you figure out where that is.

The House Raccoon

A mother told me that her youngest son had a pet raccoon in the house one summer. It did the funniest things like the following:

- Scaring the cat that was trying to let it nurse by making terrible sounds
- Holding its own bottle and purring
- Going into people's bedrooms while they were asleep and pinching their noses and biting their toes
- Swimming in the bathroom stools
- Raising out of a round bathroom trash can and touching an aunt on her bare leg (The aunt screamed, and the raccoon ran under the bed, shaking.)

- Crawling up under the dash of the car and falling into the glove compartment when he weighed about twenty pounds
- Washing his hands with soap and water and never hanging back the towel
- Wetting on the bathroom floor in Grandma's house and using her best towel to try to clean up the mess
- Eating a neighbor's pie as it was cooling in the window
- Going to a neighbor's house and swimming in their bathroom stool and then crawling into their bread drawer in the kitchen (The family had to rescue the raccoon from the neighbor's house. They had let him in to see what he would do, and the raccoon would not let them pick him up.)
- Crawling up the back of the wife's chair and kissing her on the cheek. Crawling up the mister's chair and biting him (The mister was talking to a customer one day and had to say, "Can I call you back later? I'm being attacked by a raccoon." The missus replied, "They probably think we have chickens in our house too.")
- Scaring treat-or-treaters by jumping out of the dark at them and wanting their candy
- Sitting on people's shoulders and picking pockets
- Taking pens and barrettes out of the girl's hair
- Grabbing a large bowl of popcorn and spilling it across two rooms
- Crawling into the milk truck when the milkman wasn't looking (He was sitting on top of cartons of ice cream and wouldn't let the milkman into the back of his truck at the next stop.)
- Washing all his food before he ate it
- Opening the refrigerator door and getting ice (He would wash it and then try to figure out where it went.)

- Jumping into bathtubs of water and swimming around the person trying to take a bath (All bathroom doors had to be locked.)
- Going fishing in a cousin's aquarium
- Feeling of people's hands when they felt of his
- Never knowing he was a raccoon

Bible: God put man in charge of all the animals.

Getting Even

One of the PE teachers was using a certain kind of time clock that had a funny-sounding bell on it. The bell sounded almost like a fire alarm. He decided to play a joke on the science teacher next door.

The next day, while the science students were quietly reading their assignment, the PE teacher set the time clock to go off in a few seconds and quietly placed it in the back of the science room.

The bell started ringing. The science teacher automatically grabbed her grade book to check student names and marched the class out of class and some distance from the building. She took the grade book and made sure all the students had made it out of the burning building.

The science teacher looked around and realized that her class was the only class outside. While she was trying to decide what to do, the principal came out and wanted to know if her class had started to go on an unscheduled field trip.

The science teacher was embarrassed. She realized that the PE teacher had played a joke on her. "I'll find a way to get even with him," she told herself. Three weeks later, she had her chance.

While the two teachers were conducting fourth-grade PE together, she told Mr. Joker that she had found a new exercise to help students develop their neck muscles. She explained the new exercise, "Make a funnel out of a piece of paper and tuck the funnel in the front of your sweat pants. Put a penny on your nose and see if you can drop the penny into the funnel," the science teacher said.

While the students watched, she demonstrated by making a funnel and putting it on top of Mr. Joker's sweatpants. At the same time, she sent a student into the science room for a glass of water.

While the PE teacher was trying to balance the penny on his nose so he could drop it into the funnel, the science teacher poured the glass of water down the funnel.

The PE teacher jumped and squealed. "I guess you got even with me," he said after he caught his breath.

The fourth graders returned to their classroom laughing. "It looks like Mr. PE Teacher needs to be potty-trained," they said.

Bible: "Vengeance is mine. I will repay," says the Lord.

Bewildered

Mrs. Little was teaching her sixth graders the different bases other than base ten in math. One of the best students was in a corner, looking sick. "Are you sick, John?" asked Mrs. Little.

"No! I'm not sick. I just don't know beans from buttermilk about this new stuff!" John exclaimed.

Bible: If any person lacks wisdom, let him ask of God who gives liberally and upbraideth not.

Swinging without a Rope

It had been a busy morning. Mrs. Hall was trying to rest a minute over a quick lunch. She happened to look out through the lunchroom window. On one side of the school playground was the playground teacher. On the other side of the playground were two small buildings. The buildings were at least five feet apart.

Just as Mrs. Hall looked out the window, she saw her most agile student make the jump from one building to the other. He was barely hanging on to the roof of the second building. Another of Mrs. Hall's students was perched in a jumping position on top of the first building.

Mrs. Hall ran out of the lunchroom screaming loudly. The other teachers wondered if she had finally "flipped her lid."

Mrs. Hall made it to the building in time to stop the second student from jumping and helped the first student drop to the ground.

The two students later became great football players and wrestlers. I wonder if their guardian angels worked overtime that day.

Bible: The Lord will send his angels to watch over you in case you dash your foot against a stone or fly through the air.

A Halloween Trick

Every year, at Halloween, Mr. Piper enjoyed telling his students this story. "There is an Indian princess buried northeast of town in a special place. If you go there at midnight on Halloween and say, 'Princess, Princess, what are you doing?' she will say, 'Nothing, nothing at all,'" Mr. Piper said.

The students' eyes were as big as silver dollars.

"This is true," Mr. Piper said.

The students looked at Mr. Piper, not knowing whether to believe him or not. "I wouldn't lie to you," Mr. Piper said. "Let me tell you the story again, and listen very carefully," he ordered.

After hearing the story the second time, some of the students would catch the joke and start laughing. Most of the students, however, still could imagine themselves talking to a dead Indian princess. Mr. Piper always had to tell the story several times and end up explaining the meaning. "What does the Indian princess say?" he asked.

"Nothing, nothing at all," the students answered.

"That's right. If she ever says something, then it's time to leave," Mr. Piper said.

"That's a good one," the students replied. "Now, let's find someone we can tell the story to."

Bible: It is appointed for man once to die and after that the judgment.

Oops!

It was Mr. Baldwin's first day of teaching. He wanted everything to be perfect. Mr. Baldwin had spent days in his classroom working on decorations and bulletin boards. He had a neat-looking classroom for the students that morning.

Mr. Baldwin wanted every student to be excited about starting back to school. He was trying to remember the things he had learned in his four years in college. "Act like you know everything and be very confident as you stand before your class," one of his college professors had said.

Mr. Baldwin went over his lesson plans again and tried to cover up any apprehension he was feeling.

One boy Mr. Baldwin knew well came in with a group of other students. The boy looked around and started to grin. Mr. Baldwin started to relax. Then the student commented with disgust, "Hey, Teacher, you spelled *senior* wrong on your bulletin board!"

Mr. Baldwin was terribly embarrassed.

Bible: If anyone lacks knowledge, let him ask God.

Diagnosis

One day, a first-grade girl, who had come from a mixed-up home life, walked into the classroom from recess. "I'm really tired, and I have a terrible headache. I must be pregnant," she said with a sigh.

Saying: Be careful, little ears, what you hear.

Know Everything

It was the first day of school. Lyn walked into the first-grade classroom and told his teacher, "I don't know what I'm doing here. I already know everything."

Lyn did well in school and proved he did know a lot. He won many science awards.

When his parents moved to the city, Lyn was put into a gifted program and was quite successful. I'm sure he would agree that on the first day of school, he didn't really know everything.

Bible: The Lord gives knowledge and wisdom.

The Nerve of Some Kids

It was math time. Mrs. Boggs had just handed out a difficult test. Richard hurried through the test and wanted something else to do. Mrs. Boggs told Richard how important tests are and that he should always take the time to recheck his paper. She reminded him he should always do his best.

Richard took his test paper back to his desk. He looked around the room for a few minutes and then handed the paper back to Mrs. Boggs.

"If you don't care anymore about your grade than this, I'll just go ahead and grade your paper, and you'll just get what you deserve!" Mrs. Boggs shouted.

Richard stood beside Mrs. Boggs's desk and watched her grade his paper. Mrs. Boggs was anxious to scold him about his low grade. She could hardly believe it. Richard did not miss one question or problem. He had made a perfect grade. Mrs. Boggs had to apologize.

Bible: The Lord will lead you and guide you.

Help! The Cops Are Coming!

Mr. and Mrs. Brim had been looking for a place to live in the city. They were living in a camper and were anxious to move into a house. One morning, Mr. Brim put on his best clothes and went downtown to fill the car with gas. He was gone for two hours.

When he returned, Mr. Brim told his wife what had taken him so long and the trouble he had gotten into.

While Mr. Brim was at the gas station, a man came up to him. "I have heard you are looking for a house, and I know about a house that will be just right for you," the man said.

Mr. Brim replied, "But we have already found a house. We are supposed to move into it this week."

"Just let me show you this other house, and maybe you'll change your mind," the man argued. "We can even go in my car," he said.

Mr. Brim went with the man. They stopped for coffee on the way. Just before they reached the house, the man said, "This house belongs to my girlfriend. I couldn't locate her this morning. I don't have the keys to the house, but she is so anxious to sell it that I know she won't care if we just go and look at the outside."

Mr. Brim and the man decided they could force the garage door open far enough to crawl inside and see the rest of the house. In the garage, they were attacked by two small dogs. The two men were able to escape through a side door leading to the backyard before they were bitten. The side door set off a burglar alarm. They had to get away before the police arrived.

Mrs. Brim had to laugh when she imagined how the two men must have looked rolling under the garage door while dogs were chewing on their feet.

The man called his girlfriend at work. "I found a prospective buyer for your house," he said. "Could you please come and unlock the house for us and tell the policeman in your yard that you know me and I'm not trespassing?" the man asked. "We accidentally set off your burglar alarm," he explained.

Bible: The Lord will give you a way of escape.

Twisted Tongue

Mr. Triad was talking to his friend about a new beauty shop in town. The friend replied, "It's old-fashioned to call them beauty shops. They call them beauty salons today."

Mr. Triad was telling his wife about the new beauty shop and said, "Look at that new beauty salon … sl … sl … lop!"

Bible: If we can control our tongue, we can control the whole body.

Memories of Santa Claus

Ronny was two years old when his mother took him to see Santa Claus for the first time. He started crying. "What's the matter?" his mother asked.

"I don't like him. He has scissors on his face!" Ronny cried.

Twenty-four years later, Ronny took his young son to the North Pole in Colorado to see Santa. Grandma gave Garrett two pieces of candy. "Would you like to put these in a plastic sack and take them to Santa Claus?" Grandma asked. Garrett nodded and helped Grandma put the candy in the sack.

At the North Pole, Garrett sat on Santa's lap. Santa asked Garrett what he wanted for Christmas. "I would like a game and a toy truck," Garrett answered. As Garrett crawled off Santa's lap, he handed Santa the candy.

"Oh, thank you!" Santa exclaimed. "Is it all right if I put them here on top of my fireplace until I get time to eat them later?" he asked.

"No! You can't do that because one of them is mine!" Garrett shouted.

Bible: Share with those who have not.

Thoughtful Little Boy

It was Easter Vacation. The church was having an Easter egg hunt in the yard surrounding the church and parsonage. The minister and his wife had done a lot of work in the yard and planted many flowers. Irises and tulips were blooming in several different places.

Norman was one little boy who came for the Easter egg hunt. He thought he would try to be helpful. He picked all the pretty flowers and took them to the parsonage. Norman rang the doorbell. When the preacher's wife answered the door, Norman handed her all the flowers. "I thought I would bring you all your flowers before the kids stepped on them during the hunt," he said proudly. The preacher's wife did not know whether to laugh or cry, so she did a little of both.

Bible: The Lord will remove you from danger.

When the Monsters Come Out

A thunderstorm was coming. Danny told his grandmother, "I'm not afraid of the lightning, but when it thunders, it just scares me to death."

Grandmother explained, "The lightning is the fire made when two clouds crash together, and the thunder is only the noise of what has already happened."

"That's not right, Grandma. My big brother says that all that noise is the Space Monsters we watch on TV. He said that they are outside our house, and the noise is them trying to get into our house," Danny explained.

Bible: The Lord will protect us if we but ask.

Bravery

John told his grandmother that he had been watching the Space Monsters on TV. "Doesn't it scare you?" she asked.

"Yes," John answered. Then he stood as tall as he could, stuck out his chest, and held his head high. "But I try to be brave!" John exclaimed.

Bible: The Lord will give you courage.

Shook-Up Cop

I had a friend that was rather wealthy. She was one of the first people I knew to purchase a car with electric windows. One day, she was stopped by a patrolman. She was upset and nervous.

While she was getting her driver's license out of her purse, she accidentally bumped the window button. She heard a yell and realized that she had caught the patrolman's head in the window. My friend was so frightened that she might be arrested that she started to stutter apologies.

"Never mind. Just roll your window back down," the patrolman squeaked.

My friend obeyed and waited while the law officer wrote her a citation for driving too fast. He handed the paper to my friend and walked back to his motorcycle.

My friend thought she had settled down until she realized that she had put the car into reverse instead of forward. Before she could slam on the brakes, she heard a thud behind her. As the officer picked up himself and his motorcycle, my friend crawled out of the car to apologize.

"Lady, please get out of here, and don't worry about me ever stopping you again!" the officer said.

Bible: Those who trust the Lord will never stumble.

Beauty?

A three-year-old was watching his grandmother put makeup on her face. He later told his mother, "Grandma paints her face brown every morning." "How come you don't do that?" he asked.

Bible: God will give you beauty for ashes.

What Was in the Field?

I guess it all depends on what part of the country you are from. A city teacher told me that she had just visited a field where the farmer was harvesting. It was the first time she had watched the crop gathered. This is how she described it:

"I saw this large lawnmower eating these funny-looking plants with seeds on them. Then the lawnmower went over to something that looked like a pregnant giraffe and spat up all the seeds into it. Then, while the large lawnmower went to eat more seeds, the pregnant giraffe went over and spit all the seeds into a large truck bed. The truck took the seeds to town and dumped them on the floor of a very tall skinny building. The seeds went through the holes in the floor, and I didn't see them anymore."

For city people, the large lawnmower was a combine; the pregnant giraffe, a portable dump wagon; the tall skinny building, a grain elevator.

Another farmer was checking his crop in the field. It was when the news was reporting strange things in the fields. Scorched places were found in some pastures, along with dead cattle with certain parts missing. Some people even thought it might be aliens.

As Mr. Smith looked over his crop, he could see something white in the corner of the pasture next to the field. In fact, he could see something white in each corner of his pasture. The objects had the same shape as a mummy.

Mr. Smith was shaking as he pulled back the white sheet, fearing there was a body underneath. There was nothing. He later learned that the white sheets were markers that a weed-spray pilot had put there to mark where he wanted to spray.

It is funny how one's imagination can run wild sometimes.

Bible: Things are not always what they seem.

Streaking

Some years ago, a few strange American people got a kick out of streaking. Somehow they seemed to get a thrill out of taking off all their clothes and running down the street to shock people with nothing but a ski mask on.

Mrs. Brown told her school class that streaking was terrible. She also mentioned that the Romans lost their pride in covering up their bodies, and their civilization eventually came to an end. The students started laughing.

A few days later, Mrs. Brown was walking down the school hall. She saw a new sign taped on the wall and stopped to read it. "Oh no!" she exclaimed.

In clear large letters, the sign read, "Anyone wanting to join the Hometown Streaking Club, sign here." Every teacher's name had been signed in different but bold large handwriting that looked official.

Mrs. Brown pulled the sign down and took it to Mr. Reed's room for him to see. "Oh my gosh, I didn't know what those girls borrowed my tape for!" he exclaimed. "I'm glad that no other teacher or the principal or any parents saw the sign before you took it down, Mrs. Brown!" Mr. Reed exclaimed.

The kids thought it was funny since a couple of the teachers were rather old and would not have made very good streakers.

Later the same week, the community traveled to a neighboring state for a basketball game. It was in the middle of the second quarter. The score was tied with twenty points for each team.

The other team had just made two points, and one of the home team's best players was dribbling the ball to the other end of the court. The buzzer sounded, and everyone thought the other coach had sent in two new players, but these two players seemed to be wearing tan suits.

The player who was dribbling the basketball let the ball go, bouncing across the floor to the other team. He was standing frozen, with his mouth dropped open, watching the two new players.

The other team grabbed the ball and made two easy points. The two new "players" did not have any clothes on. They had ski masks over their heads. The two men ran the length of the gym toward the pep club and band and disappeared through a door at the end of the gym.

The gym became quiet. Then someone in the crowd said, "It would have been funny if that door had been locked, and the two men could not have run out of the building!" Everyone laughed.

The team lost by one point. Was this a fair victory?

Bible: Adam and Eve used fig leaves to cover themselves.

Don't Say That!

One of my friends and her husband raise registered cattle and horses. One day, we were in town together, discussing if we needed to go to the grocery store or not. "Don't let me ever hear you say that again!" my friend shouted at me.

"Say what?" I asked.

"That you want to go downtown and get bread!" she snapped back at me.

From that time on, I have always said, "I need to buy a loaf of bread."

Bible: Jesus is the bread of life.

Unfunny Days

It was toward the last day of school. Joey hurt his arm playing outside before the first class bell rang. Mrs. Bay took him to the principal's office, and the nurse took Joey to the doctor. Two hours later, Joey returned with his arm in a large cast.

During the noon recess, Sammy fell off the monkey bars. Her arm was broken, and the bone was protruding out of the skin. Another doctor's trip.

Elizabeth fell across a jumping hurdle in PE, bruising the lower half of her body. X-rays showed her kidneys were bruised. She missed several days of school. What a day!

The next week, Henry was swinging on the monkey bars and hit his head on one of them. His head looked like it had a goose egg on it. Mrs. Bay tried to put an ice pack on it, but Henry just wanted to be left alone.

His pupils were not dilated, so Mrs. Bay let him stay in school. The next day, Henry's mother came to school angry. Henry had a hairline crack in his skull.

"I can't write today because I hurt my hand, Mrs. Bay," Bobby said.

Mrs. Bay checked Bobby's hand. It was terribly swollen. "When did you do this?" she asked.

"At home last night," Bobby answered.

"I think you need to go to the doctor this evening after school. It looks like some of your fingers might be broken," Mrs. Bay said.

The next day, Bobby's hand was even more swollen. He told Mrs. Bay that he had not been to the doctor. Mrs. Bay sent him to the school nurse. The nurse took Bobby to the hospital. X-rays showed two broken fingers.

Mrs. Bay's class went skating for their last-day-of-school party. Lizzy fell right in front of Mrs. Bay and broke her leg. What a year!

Judy cut her arm. The next day, she showed it to her teacher. "You need to let a doctor see this. It might be serious," the teacher said.

"My parents have looked at it," Judy replied.

The teacher was confused by the remark until she learned that both of Judy's parents were doctors.

Everyone was ready for summer vacation.

Bible: The Lord will bind up your wounds.

A Teacher's Story

For years, Mr. Bing started his school day with prayer. He prayed that the students be given the wisdom to learn and that the teachers would be given the wisdom to teach without confusion.

Mr. Bing taught social studies and showed videos. Because of this, the special-education students were kept in Mr. Bing's class for part of the day.

One day, Mr. Bing asked a special-education student, Charles, to read out of the textbook, expecting to help Charles with most of the words. Mr. Bing was surprised when Charles read as well as half the kids in the regular class.

Mr. Bing was angry. "Charles, you can read better than many kids in this class. I think you have been pretending to be dumb so you won't have to do a lot of schoolwork," he said. "I want you to know that if you ever fail another one of my classes, I will spank you, and when I assign homework, you better do it!" he shouted.

Charles made passing grades for the rest of the year.

That summer, Mr. Bing was talking to Charles's mother. "I want you to know that God healed my son's mind when you prayed for him in school. Thank you," Charles's mother said.

Mr. Bing was embarrassed. It had never crossed his mind that was why Charles had been able to read and do his assignments.

The next year, the principal called Mr. Bing into his office. "Mr. Bing, I want you to know that you are breaking the state law by praying in class," the principal said. Then he said, "Don't take me wrong. I'm not against prayer. In fact, my favorite teachers when I was in school were those who prayed. But the laws are different now, and you are breaking the law. I want you to know that if there is any trouble from any parents or only one parent, we can't stand behind you at all. I firmly advise you to stop before there is any trouble," he warned.

The next morning, after the bell rang, Mr. Bing started his class. "Teacher, you forgot to pray," one student said.

"I didn't forget. We just aren't going to be able to pray anymore," Mr. Bing said.

"Why?" one student asked.

"We need to pray," another student said.

These were children who rarely went to church.

"I agree with you, but it is against the law to pray in school. It could cause trouble for the principal if any of your parents complained," Mr. Bing answered. "We must obey the laws of our country," he said.

Jamie held up her hand and asked, "Teacher, if we are ever hit by an atom bomb, would it be all right to break the law and pray in school then?"

Mr. Bing did not know how to answer the question.

Bible: With prayer and thanksgiving, let your requests be made known to God.

Jump the Car

Four-year-old Garrett enjoyed watching the *Dukes of Hazzard* on TV. Garrett and his parents were coming back to town from checking cattle when they saw a car along the side of the road. They were some of their friends.

Mr. Sharp walked over to the car and said, "Ronny, my car stopped, and I can't get it started. Could you jump my car with your truck? I think my battery must be low," he explained.

Ronny put his battery cables on each vehicle and helped Mr. Sharp start his car. When the family was ready to go on home, Garrett started to cry.

"What's the matter?" Garrett's mother asked.

"I wanted to see Daddy jump that car," Garrett said.

Bible: We shall mount up with wings like angels.

Scary Slumber Party

Gary was eight years old in August. His mother let him celebrate by inviting eight friends to go swimming. After the swimming party and picnic, the eight boys were invited to stay for a "slumber party." The boys slept in sleeping bags in the garage that night.

Gary's mother heard the boys talking through the bathroom window.

"I think I heard something out there in the yard," a voice said.

"I think I see a light over there in the yard," another voice said.

"I think there is a wolf out there," a third voice said.

"I'm scared," Gary's mother heard several boys say.

The high-school boy from next door had just come home from a date. He thought he heard an unusual noise next door and went over to investigate. He heard whispering in his neighbor's garage. "What's going on in here?" the neighbor boy shouted.

Gary's mother heard the boys screaming as they ran into the house. She heard the neighbor boy say, "Gee whiz, I didn't mean to scare you," By then, he was talking to an empty garage.

Gary's mother went into the kitchen to see if the boys were all right. She had to laugh when she saw the young boys with nothing on but their shorts, trying to hide behind one another and not wanting to go back outside.

Bible: Trust in the Lord, and He will take care of you.

Keep It Even

A six-year-old was asked, "Are you going to have a baby brother next spring?"

"Nope!" was the answer.

"A sister?"

"No," the child answered again.

"Then what are you going to have?" the child was asked.

"One of each. We have to keep our family even," the child explained.

What Time Is It?

A young mother was working in the bedroom one morning. Her three-year-old son was helping her. "Johnny, I want you to go to the kitchen and see what time it is," Johnny's mother said.

Johnny ran to the kitchen. "It's thirty o'clock!" he yelled.

"Where is the big hand?" Johnny's mother asked.

There was no answer. Finally, Johnny came back into the bedroom. "Here is the big hand," he said and handed his mother a large oven glove.

Bible: The Lord will hold you by your right hand.

We Haven't Met Yet

Grandpa and Grandma were taking five-year-old Ronny to the hospital to meet his new baby brother. They stopped by a gas station on the way.

"How do you like that baby brother of yours?" a friend asked.

"I don't know because I haven't met him yet," Ronny answered.

Ronny's family was surprised when he ran into the hospital and said, "I have a present for my baby brother" and tried to put a package of gum in the baby's hand.

They became good friends. Years later, Ronny was bringing Danny home from school one evening in his "new" car. They were late because they had an accident. Another car had run into them.

The patrolman was called. He took both drivers' stories and gave Ronny a ticket. Danny was angry when he saw his brother get the ticket and fine. He was still angry when the two boys came home. "But a person does have the right-of-way when they come out of an alley, don't they, Mom?" he asked their mother.

Bible: The Lord will hold you by His right hand.

Sunburn

A six-year-old was watching her grandmother put on her makeup. "Why do you put that brown stuff on your face?" she asked.

"To make me look better and to keep me from getting sunburned," the grandmother answered.

"I think you need to put some of it on the back of your neck too. It looks sunburned," the child replied.

Bible: The Lord is our protection in the day of trouble.

The City

The Wilsons took Grandma on her first trip to the city. Grandma was excited and saw many things for the first time. She had never stayed in a hotel before. The bellhop took Grandma's suitcase and started up the stairs.

Grandma ran after him and grabbed her suitcase. Then she ran across the lobby and told Mr. Wilson, "Son, we have to watch the people in this place. That young man in the funny suit tried to steal my suitcase."

Later that evening, the Wilsons were sitting in their car, watching the people go by. Grandma saw a bright Mixed Drinks sign in one of the windows on the street. "Son, what are Mexican drinks?" she asked.

Bible: The Lord will bless through generations.

Houses on the Mountain

Jim and Sally were living in a nice mountain area next to a large city. All the houses were required to be earth colors so as not to destroy the scenery with bright colors.

Jim's mother, Agnes, came to visit. "It looks like people who can afford fancy large houses like these could afford to paint them," she said.

Jim, Sally, and Agnes went to see a new house that had just been built on a steep side of the mountain. The balcony was hanging over a valley below with a drop-off of about two hundred feet.

"Oh, what a beautiful view," Sally said.

"Yes, it is, but watch that first step. It's a dandy!" Agnes exclaimed.

Bible: The angels will hold you lest you dash your foot against a stone.

A What?

It was reported several years ago that Senators William B. Spong and Hiram Fong got their heads together to sponsor a bill recommending the mass ringing of the church bells to hail the arrival in Hong Kong of the U.S. table tennis team after its tour of Communist China.

The motion died, cheating Congress out of passing the Spong-Fong Hong Kong Ping-Pong Ding-Dong Bell bill.

Front Seat

A Sunday-school teacher was teaching the children the Lord's Prayer. The new part was "Thy will be done." "Do you know what a backseat driver is?" the teacher asked.

One child answered, "Yes, I know. It is when it's too hard to drive from the front seat."

Pots and Pans

A six-year-old was looking at a Corning top kitchen stove. She exclaimed, "I like this stove, but where are the wires? Where do you put your pans?"

Bible: Unless you become like little children, you can't enter the kingdom of heaven.

An Eventful Weekend

Pam Smith and her two sons—Ronny was fourteen, and Danny was nine—traveled across the state to visit two of Pam's cousins. Ronny took his friend Dale along. It was a weekend with relatives that they would never forget.

The first evening, Dale broke his collarbone when he and Ronny had a wreck on one of his cousin's motorbikes.

The next day, one of the cousin's daughters was run over by a horse that the kids were riding. Thankfully, she only had cuts and bruises.

On the third day, the cousins took their guests fishing at a large lake near their home. Danny fell off a cliff and into a deep part of the lake.

"Danny can't swim!" Pam shouted to Cousin Kay.

Kay was pulling off his shoes to rescue Danny when he looked out at the lake. "Well, he is swimming!" Kay exclaimed.

Danny swam to safety and crawled out of the lake in about two feet of mud. But he happened to have been wearing his new school shoes. The shoes were retrieved but were in a terrible mess.

Pam and the boys started home the next day. She stopped in a small town in the northern part of the state to buy some gas. She discovered she had left her purse at the house of one of her cousins and had no money or credit cards. The gas station attendant sold Pam a tank full of gas on credit with no identification.

In another small town, Pam and the boys were hungry. They stopped at a small café, and Pam asked the waitress if she would sell them some dinner on credit. "I don't think we can do that since we don't know you," the waitress said.

Pam did not know what to do until she heard someone behind her say, "I know this lady, and I will pay the bill if she doesn't."

Pam turned around to see a friend she had not seen for years.

"I know this guy, so I'll credit you with all the meals you need," the waitress said with a smile.

God helped Pam and the boys travel all day with all their needs met. The gas station didn't even send them a bill, and Pam had to call them about it.

Bible: My God will supply all your needs according to His riches in Christ Jesus.

Changed to the Wall

I called to obtain information from a friend. Her young child answered the phone. I asked, "Is your mother there?"

"No," she answered.

"Is your sister there?" I asked.

"Yes, but she is outside," the child replied.

"Can you get her so I can talk to her?" I asked.

"I can't. I'm chained to the wall!" she exclaimed. The portable phone was not working, and she was using the landline, the one "chained to the wall."

Bible: The Lord will break every chain.

Believe Anything?

An eight-year-old, Kris, was spending a few days with her grandparents. They had just sat down to supper when Grandpa asked how Grandma had broken the windshield on the car. A bird had hit the windshield where a rock had already damaged it. "It's a long story," Grandmother said.

"I'll believe anything," Grandpa replied.

Just then, Kris said, "Grandpa, that pitcher will walk across the table."

"What!" Grandpa exclaimed.

"Well, Grandpa, you said you would believe anything," Kris said with a giggle.

When Kris was five years old, she told her grandpa that she was three feet and seven inches tall and weighed forty pounds.

"That's hard to believe," Grandpa said.

"Well, then, I must be seven feet and three inches tall, but I'm sure that I weigh forty pounds."

God says, "Those that come to me must believe I am, and I am a rewarder of those that seek me."

When?

Mrs. Wilson asked her friend's young daughter what day they bought their new vehicle. The young girl answered, "The day before tomorrow."

Who Did It?

Mrs. Terry was giving Nicole her piano lesson while Ki was waiting for hers. "You need to practice, Nicole, like Ki does," Mrs. Terry said. "Don't you, Ki?" she asked.

Ki turned around from playing on the computer. "No, I think that that's my sister you are talking about," she replied, rather confused.

Bible: Honesty pays.

Who Is Speaking?

Mr. Rosengrant was teaching his first-grade class when he was called to the office to answer a telephone call. He told his class to be quiet and keep reading.

When he reached the office, he knew little Suzy would be out of her seat by then. Mr. Rosengrant picked up the intercom and said, "Suzy, sit back down in your seat!"

Another teacher had stopped her work to check in on Mr. Rosengrant's students, knowing that he had been called to the telephone. He heard the message over the intercom, and he also heard little Suzy say, "Yes, God."

Bible: When we call, the Lord will answer.

The Farm

A family had a chicken farm, along with a garden and some other animals. One day, they received an order for twenty baby chickens. The little daughter, Sarah, wanted to help with the tiny, cute baby chickens. She kept saying, "Daddy, what can I do? Daddy, what can I do?"

Finally, the father needed to feed and water the chickens, so he said, "You can name the baby chickens for me."

"Okay, Daddy," Sarah said and started naming the babies.

When her father returned, little Sarah was crying.

"What's the matter?" he asked, picking up his small daughter.

"I'm sorry, Daddy, but I ran out of names," the child sobbed.

Bible: We will be rewarded for doing our best.

The farmer had three older children who helped with the work. One day, they did not do their chores, so the farmer made them hoe in the garden for not doing what they were told.

Sarah watched the other kids hoeing the garden. It looked like they were having fun, and she was left out again. She walked up to her father, stomped her feet, and said, "I'm not doing my chores, and I'm not doing anything you tell me to do today!"

The father was laughing because he knew why she had said she would not obey. She wanted to be with the other kids.

Bible: God said we would never be alone.

What Time?

"Grandma, will you and Grandpa come to my Bible quiz next Saturday?" Aron asked over the telephone.

"What time is your quiz next Saturday?" Grandma asked.

"It's at noon thirty!" Aron answered.

Warm-Up?

It was late October when Alan came to take his piano lesson. He asked if he could play his warm-up scales first. A warm-up scale is an exercise to help the fingers to be more limber. After Alan played the warm-up song, he said, "It didn't work. I'm still cold."

The teacher decided it was time to turn on the furnace.

Bible: It is warm in the sunshine of God's love.

What Is the Weather?

It was starting to snow. Dan and Donna checked the weather on the TV and the computer. The computer said, "Weather tonight ... partly sunny."

You're What?

Here is the way some single men introduce themselves on the computer:

- Hi. I am a rich, muscled six-foot-four-inch man trapped in a poor five-foot-six body with no money in the bank. Will someone please help me?
- I am a great catch, although I don't want to compare myself to a bass.

Bible: The Lord will give you the right mate.

A Ninety-Two-Year-Old Friend

Darlene: My eighty-two-year-old boyfriend is going to take care of my little dog when I move to heaven.

Grace: I think you will probably outlive Bob.

Darlene: You really think so?

Grace: Yes, the Bible tells about some people living to be 120, and I think you have a good chance of doing that.

Darlene: Oh dear, I hope my car lasts that long.

Grace and Darlene usually sat on the front pew for church. One day, Grace had to leave early, so she sat on the back pew. Darlene quickly walked back to where Grace was sitting. "I see that you have backslidden," Darlene said loud enough for everyone to hear.

One Sunday, Reverend Taylor was preaching. He asked, "Have you ever known someone who talks a lot and goes on and on?"

Darlene pointed her finger at Reverend Taylor and loudly said, "Yes, you!"

Reverend Taylor had to take a few minutes to laugh before he could continue with his message.

There is a message taped on the mirror in Darlene's living room. It reads, "The speed limit in this facility is five miles an hour, not fifty-five miles an hour."

Bible: The Lord blesses the elderly.

A Matter of Spelling

Braxton was helping his mother take down the Christmas decorations in her classroom. "We cannot have this!" Braxton exclaimed.

After the third time he said that, his mother stopped working and walked across the room. She asked, "What can we not have?"

"We can't have these Satan decorations!" Braxton exclaimed, holding up a large box filled with Christmas decorations.

"Oh," Braxton's mother said, "the box is labeled *satin decorations*, not *Satan decorations*."

Bible: Let the children come to me and forbid them not.

The News

Today Mr. David Smith is suing his wife, Lori Smith, for a divorce because he thinks that his wife is trying to kill him to collect on his life insurance.

It all started when the Smiths were taking a vacation. They were starting home, pulling their travel trailer. David had driven many hours and decided to let Lori drive for a while so he could rest.

Although it was against the law, he crawled into the travel trailer to rest and then decided to take a shower. He had just come out of the shower when he felt the trailer stop. He peeked through the door when Lori started up quickly, and David fell out.

The police quickly arrested him because he was naked. Lori hated to admit that David was her husband when the police caught up with her on the highway with David in the police car.

Later, Lori talked David into repairing the roof. The roof was rather steep, so he tied a rope around the bumper of the truck and the other end around his waist on the other side of the peaked roof.

Lori came out and took off in the truck. David was pulled over the top of the house and to the ground on the other side. Lori called 911, and David ended up spending some time in the hospital.

When David got out of the hospital, he didn't know that Lori had poured paint thinner on the hall bathroom stool when she cleaned up his painting mess. He lit a cigar and threw the match into the stool. There was an explosion, and now David is afraid to go home after he gets out of the hospital this time. He is still wondering if Lori is trying to kill him because he has a large life insurance policy.

Bible: Healing comes from the Lord.

What Do You Like?

Four-year-old Adyn had just completed playing soccer and had his second game of tee-ball. Great-Grandmother asked, "Adyn, which do you like more: tee-ball or soccer?"

Adyn looked at Grandma, thought for a minute, and said, "I like Shelby." Shelby was another four-year-old on his team.

Bible: Honesty always pays.

Kids

Kids are so thoughtful they can spoil you. When I first started teaching, I received so many Christmas gifts I was humbled. I appreciated each gift and said so.

Maybe it was kind of like the poor woman in the Bible who gave all she had in the offering in the church where Jesus was watching.

One boy came from a better home. He brought some expensive perfume. He placed it on my desk and said, "You better enjoy this because it costs a lot."

Another boy brought in a box of homemade candy and said, "I hope you like this because my mother wouldn't let me have a bite, so can I have a piece now?"

One morning, I went to the hospital with terrible pain instead of going to school. The doctor gave me a shot to put me to sleep for a couple of hours. When I woke up, there were get-well cards and flowers on the table beside my bed. How did my students know that I was in the hospital and bought the cards and flowers for me that morning when they had not even had recess yet?

One day, I was reviewing my class on fractions the day before their test. One young man was having a hard time coming up with the answers as quickly as some of the students. I gave a problem and asked for the answer. Alan quickly knew the answer. He held up his hand, very excited.

"Yes, Alan," I said.

"Two terds!" he shouted. He was so embarrassed he had to leave the class when the class started laughing.

More Special Thoughts

When my sons were growing up, we had a trampoline to play on. We had this one game where two would be on the trampoline together. One would sit with legs crossed and hands holding their ankles. The other one would bounce the sitting one higher and higher until they turned loose of their ankles.

My 180-pound son was bouncing me, and I thought I could take one more bounce before I turned loose. The first thing I knew, I was flying through the air and landed on my head in the middle of the trampoline. "I'm sorry, Mom. I would have caught you if I knew where you were coming down," my son said.

I seemed to be all right, except I had a stiff neck for the next couple of weeks. Two years later, my arm began to hurt. Sometimes it felt like boiling water was poured on it.

It became so painful that I finally went to the doctor. I can remember pushing my back against the wall of my classroom to relieve the pain. The X-rays did not show any problems, so the local doctor sent me to a large hospital in a larger town.

I had to take a shot of iodine before the X-rays. I was waiting on a rollaway bed. It was very, very cold when I fainted. It seemed I was in a hole in the ground going around and around when I heard two men yelling, "Breathe, lady, breathe!" I opened my eyes and was aware of the men shaking me. The doctor was called and said I was allergic to iodine and to never take it again.

The X-rays showed two broken bones in my neck that were rubbing together and pinching the nerves in my arm. I was scheduled for surgery. The doctors took out a small piece of bone from my hip to replace the broken bones. The only pain I had after surgery was when I got up from the table and bumped my hip on the edge.

I was able to go back to teaching in a couple of weeks, but I had lost my voice because the surgery was done from the front of my neck instead of going in from the back and operating close to my spinal cord. When the doctors pushed my esophagus out of the way, it caused me to lose my voice. I had to whisper to my students, and they ended up whispering back to me, or one of the students would be "my voice" during the day. We had a very quiet classroom for a while and did not get behind our schedule.

This is what happened the first day I was back in school.

The day had gone pretty well. That afternoon, the principal called me into his office. When I got there, he ignored me for what seemed like a long time. I finally said, "I have a class, and I can't wait any longer."

"I think someone is looking for you in the science room," the principal finally said.

I thought he was acting rather strange but didn't say anything. I hurried to the science room. I did not want to disturb the class, so I quietly slipped in. Was I ever surprised! The desks were covered with white paper and decorations everywhere. There were three large signs that read WELCOME BACK TO SCHOOL, TEACHER. There was even a special chair for me to sit in. Just as we were getting ready to enjoy homemade cookies and Kool-Aid, my laughing principal joined us.

Later that week, the principal called me into his office again. This time, I dismissed my students for the day. Instead of ignoring me, he seemed upset. I wondered what I had done wrong. He ignored me for a few minutes and said, "You better check the science room again."

This time, I thought one of my students was in trouble. When I was close to the science-room door, I could smell good things to eat. I was almost afraid to open the door, and I thought about running. I slipped through the door again and saw refreshments and gifts. I tried to stay in the back of the room and thought, "They are having a shower for someone, and I don't remember what or who it is for, and I did not bring a gift."

The party was for me. I had gotten married the week before, and the teachers and administrators were giving me an "undies" shower. Can you believe it? I was forty-five years and starting my second marriage, and those people made me feel as important as a young new bride.

Bible: Treat each other the way you want to be treated.

I Know Why It Does That!

Jean was visiting with her friend and family at a resort in the mountains. They were looking through a ghost town and an old schoolhouse. There was an outhouse nearby. Six-year-old Samuel came running to the rest of the family.

"Ms. Jean, Ms. Jean," he shouted, "the guy who built this little house did not know what he was doing! It stinks!"

Bible: The father kissed his runaway son even when he smelled like pigs.

What's Up?

As long as there are young people, there will be things to laugh about. I just received a letter from my daughter-in-law that told me about my grandson's first week in school. He said, "I haven't gotten into trouble yet, but Jeff has."

When I asked about eating at school, he said, "I sat beside the boy with sharp teeth."

When he was four, he came in from the yard and told his mother, "I have been outside talking to God."

"That's great," said his mother.

The child continued, "I asked him if it was going to snow tomorrow, and he said yes."

"It can't snow tomorrow!" his mother exclaimed.

"Why not?" my grandson asked.

"It would kill all the plants in the garden and the flowers around the house," his mother tried to explain.

"Oh, we can't let that happen. I better hurry up and go back and tell God to change His plans for tomorrow," the child said confidently.

When asked about the difference between preschool and kindergarten, he said, "Preschool only had two recesses, but kindergarten has two recesses in the large space and two recesses in the small space."

Bible: Tell God your wants and plans.

Sports

It is difficult to tell how good a child will be in sports when they are young. When my son was two years old, he received his first football. He would stand on our back porch and yell at the older kids, "You can't take my football away from me!" Then I would hear him shouting a short time later, "Mom, they took my football away from me!"

By the time he was in the seventh grade, he was large for his age; and in his first year in football, he was placed playing on the line instead of the backfield. He did a great job making tackles on the line for the next four years.

At the beginning of his junior year of high school, he informed us that he was going to try out for the backfield because he was not getting along with the line coach. "If I don't make it, I guess I will just quit football," he said.

After a lot of practice, he was given the starting position as one of the halfbacks. He told me, "Mom, I should do well this year because I have a brick wall in front of me to help me get through the line."

He was talking about a friend who would be blocking players for him to give him room to run.

The first game was ready to start. His father and I were wondering how well our son would do in this new position. We were pretty nervous. We started to relax a little when he scored his first touchdown and a little more when he scored his second. More? Yes, he had three touchdowns in his first game.

We had made a double garage into a family room. There was room enough for the team to sit and wait for time for the bus to leave. One of the players played the guitar and sang. It became a place to relax before catching the bus and playing the game.

One evening, my husband came home and said, "I want to leave early so we can do some shopping along the way."

"But the team is in the family room," I said.

"It will be okay to leave now and just let Ronny lock the house when he leaves," he said.

"I don't think it is a good idea since the cheerleaders are here too," I explained.

"They are not old enough for girls to be here too," my husband said.

"They are teenagers, you know," I replied.

The team won all their games that year. The last game was between them and their biggest rival, a town twenty miles away. I expected them to be somewhat confident until I heard them talking. The opposing team had not lost a game either.

"What if they figure out our passing game?" one player said.

"What if they figure out our defense?" another player said.

It was time to board the bus to the other town. The team was nervous.

The other team came running onto the field, yelling, "Kill, kill!"

The home team felt a little better when they had the first score over the second-best team in the league. They held the other team to no score on their first possession of the ball. The home team scored again on a long pass and run. They held the other team scoreless.

The score ended up 60–0. I found out later one reason the team was so nervous. Several fathers of the players had one-hundred-dollar bets with the dads of the opposing team. They wagered that our team would prevent the rivals from scoring even one first down. "People don't look at us as a football team but something to gamble on," one player said.

It seemed there was always something to laugh about, like the time in practice the coach sent the small halfback around the right side and one of the 250-pound linemen to stop him going around to the left. They collided, and the small halfback was knocked out. The lineman started crying, "I killed him. I killed him."

One time, my son came in from practice. It was dark, and we were watching TV in the family room. "Hey, Dad, do we have health insurance?" he asked.

"Yes, son, we do, but I don't want to discuss it now. I am watching my favorite program," Dad answered.

"But I have to know about it now," my son pretested.

"Why now?" Dad asked.

"Because I ran into another player this evening in practice, and the doctor has just put nine stitches above my eye."

Some relatives drove a great distance to see one of the games. The family noticed that they were yelling at the wrong time. The family asked why they were doing that. "We just felt sorry for the other team," they answered.

Feel sad for people who don't have the Lord in their lives.

Black Stories

Eight-year-old Jack was with his father when he heard someone say that a certain person was black. He asked his father what that meant, and Jack's father asked him what color he thought they were.

Jack looked at his hands for a minute and thought. "Pink" was his reply.

Elmer was a 104-year-old member of a very large church. One day, he wanted to visit with his pastor and had to wait in line for forty minutes. The pastor asked him why he didn't sit in one of the chairs in the hall.

"Oh, I will do that when I get old" was the reply.

"Well, you do not look like you are 104," the pastor said.

Elmer laughed and said, "Black don't crack!"

Bible: God loves everyone. He is not a respecter of persons.

Cupid

Mrs. T was teaching sixth-grade math. She had students taking turns doing long divisions on the chalkboard. She was explaining a certain step to the students. When she turned around, Johnny had written on the board, "Brenda + Bobby."

"John," Mrs. T said, "We do not need things like that written on the board. If we need a Cupid, we will call on you."

The students started laughing and couldn't stop.

After class, Mrs. T asked a couple of girls what was so funny. One of the girls replied, "When you said what you did about calling on Johnny if we need a Cupid, we all imagined what Johnny would look like standing in front of the class with nothing but a ribbon on."

"That is why Johnny was so embarrassed," Mrs. T said with a chuckle. "I doubt if he will do that again," she said.

When I was in college, one science professor was very fat. He probably weighed 350 pounds. It was funny when he told this story in class.

"Acid can do many things," he said. "I was traveling once and had a bottle of acid in the back of my station wagon. My suit was hanging up back there too. Somehow, the bottle fell over and leaked on my suit without me knowing it. I checked my suit, and it seemed to be all right. I rolled down the window, so the wind could make the smell evaporate."

Two days later, I drove to a banquet where I was asked to speak. When I walked to the front, I noticed that my suit felt loose. I didn't know that my pant legs had come apart until I lifted my hand and my sleeve fell off. Everyone was laughing by the time I finished my talk and my suit was in pieces. I'm glad it was a men's meeting. The acid destroyed the thread in my suit and not the fabric, which was double-knit. I guess it was a great science lesson for me."

Bible: God will help us to "keep us from falling apart."

We were in music class one day, and the professor was teaching us how to recognize the sound of different instruments. He played a part of his tape and asked, "What kind of instrument is this?"

"A brass instrument," one student answered.

"Very good. It has a brassy sound," the professor said.

He played the next segment of the tape. "What kind of instrument is this?" he asked.

One student replied, "A woodwind."

"Yes, you can hear the woody sound," the professor said.

The students listened to the next sound, which was the sound of a guitar. "What kind of instrument is this?" he asked.

"A string instrument," another student said.

"Yes, because it has a ... a ..." the professor started to say.

By this time, the whole class was laughing. Was the professor going to say that it has a stringy sound?

One thing I remember from French class was how to say *commence*. In English, it is *kick a mouse*.

One of my best teachers was a preacher's wife. One day, she heard cursing in her class. The next day, she wrote on the whiteboard, "Cursing is a crutch for a conversational cripple."

Football in School

Don was from a farming family in the community. Most of the community was very interested in sports, but Don's family lived a long way out of town and usually did not attend sports events.

When Don was in the seventh grade, he decided that he wanted to play middle-school football. It was the first game against another team. The game was almost over, and the home team was five yards from the goal line. When the starting halfback was injured, the coach put Don in place of the injured player.

The quarterback thought he could carry the ball across the goal line for a score when he saw two players from the other team running at him. He tossed the ball to Don.

Don was surprised when he caught the ball. "What shall I do? What shall I do?" he shouted at the coach.

Just then, a player tackled Don, pushing him backward and across the goal line. The game was over, and everyone was celebrating Don's score and the win. He really didn't now know what he had done and what had happened.

The high-school team was playing a really tough team. Ronald was recovering from a very hard tackle, and his nose was bleeding. The coach had not realized Ronald had been injured. "Where is Ron?" the coach yelled, planning to send him back into the game.

"Right here, ready to go in, sir," Ron responded.

One incident in football was not funny. My youngest son and his team had just been issued new football jerseys. The team looked really cool as they huddled for their first game.

"Mom, could you fix my new jersey? I got it torn in the game last night," my son said.

"I'll try, but I don't know how to work with stretchy material," I replied.

I thought it was odd that the tear had a straight edge. "I think it has been cut," I said. I called the coach and told him about the cut in the jersey.

"There is no way the jersey has been cut," the coach said.

After more mothers called the coach with the same report, he decided maybe he should check into it. He called the coach of the other team and told him what they had found.

"That's impossible, but I will see if I can find out what happened," the other coach promised.

The night of the team's next game, the coach made a search of all the gear of his team. He found that two of his players had driven razor blades into the soles of their shoes. The players were suspended for the rest of the season.

"I am not going to let Steve walk home with me anymore after football practice," John told his mother.

"Did you guys have a fight?" his mother asked.

"No. It's not permanent. I just told him he couldn't come home with me until he starts taking a shower after practice," John replied.

"I know what you are talking about. Remember when I told you and your brother that I don't mind washing your football and basketball suits as long as you leave your bag open until I get to them the next morning," Mother reminded John.

An eighth grader broke his leg at the beginning of summer vacation and missed the summer baseball season. He had the braces off in time to play football that fall.

In the first football game, he was tackled hard by a player on the other team and fell on his arm.

It was easy to tell that his arm was broken. He began to cry loudly.

"The doctor will soon be here and make you feel better, so quit crying and act like a man," said the coach.

"I'm not crying because I hurt. I'm crying because I won't be able to play any more football this year either!" the young man yelled.

My son had a football buddy who was quite comical. Three things I remember my younger son had just brought in two cans of pop for his brother and friend. When my son's friend finished his pop, he put the can to his mouth and tapped on the can.

"What are you doing?" my son asked.

"I am trying to get the piece of ice from the can."

"Oh, that's not a piece of ice. That is the tab from the can. I have a habit of pulling it off and dropping it into the can," my son said.

"I'm glad I was not able to get it out of the can and take a chance of swallowing it," the friend said.

Birt had a father who liked to play jokes on people. One day, when he was visiting at our house, he saw a small dog's vomit on the floor. Thinking it was his dad's fake one, he kicked it. He looked at his foot and groaned. "Can someone get me a paper towel, please?" he exclaimed.

The football team was gathered at the Thompsons' house, waiting to catch the bus to the game that night. Mrs. Thompson was going through the mail. "Here is a letter for our dog, Velvet, all the way from California!" she exclaimed. "The letter says that Velvet is an official member of the Walt Disney Club since we left her in a kennel there while we were at the park."

"That dog gets more important mail than we do," several players said.

How Much Will It Cost?

—— ✠ ——

"Then God created the heavens and the earth and Adam." He said it is not good for man to be alone, so He told Adam, "I will make you a helpmate. She will cook you meals, wash your clothes, clean your house, have and raise your children, and make you comfortable in every way."

"What will this cost me? Adam asked.

"An arm and a leg," the Lord answered.

Adam thought for a moment and asked, "What can I get for a rib?" he asked.

Should I Do It Again?

Deloris and Betty were doing some volunteer work together. Betty came into the room and said, "Excuse me!"

"What did you do?" Deloris asked.

"I burped," Betty said.

"I'm sorry, but I didn't hear it," said Deloris. "You will have to do it again."

"Oh dear, I don't know if I can do it like the first time," Betty replied. "What am I saying …"

Don't Judge

———— ⊨◆⊟ ————

Mr. Bankcroft had a bad habit of judging people until, one night, he had a dream. He dreamed he went to heaven. He started looking around. "I didn't think Mrs. Baker would make it to heaven!" he exclaimed when he saw his old neighbor at the pearly gates. "And I didn't think Dean Shotner or Jack Downer would make it either," he said, surprised. Then he asked, "Why is everyone looking at me?"

Bible: Judge not that ye be not judged.

In Remembrance

The Bennit family had just returned from the funeral of a dear friend. The minister who had spoken gave arrows to the widow to give to the grandchildren for them to keep in memory of their grandfather. It was to remind them how straight their grandfather lived his life for the Lord.

Amy Bennit said, "Mom, when we have your funeral, we can tell people how much you loved cats and give everyone a kitten to remember you with. Wouldn't that make everyone happy?"

The Smartest Man in the World

A priest, doctor, preacher, the smartest man in the world, and a small boy were flying to a certain destination when the engine quit and the plane started descending. The preacher, who was also the pilot, said, "We only have four parachutes."

"I have to use one of them," the priest said. "I have people in my church who are depending on me to marry and bury them." He took one of the parachutes and jumped out.

"I have to use the next one," the doctor said. "I have sick people depending on me." He also jumped from the plane.

"I need one because people are depending on me to make new discoveries," the smartest man in the world said. Then he jumped.

"I know you have your life before you, young man, and maybe my church can get along without me," the preacher pilot said.

"We don't have to worry," the young lad replied. "When the smartest man in the world said what he did, he grabbed my backpack when he jumped out. So we both still have a parachute to jump with."

Bible: Knowledge comes from the Lord.

One I Like

Mr. Jones had a vision that he was in heaven talking to God. "I have an awfully heavy cross to carry," he whined. "Can I trade it for a smaller one?" he asked.

God showed him a room full of crosses, and Mr. Jones chose a small one. "I think I can carry this one," he said.

God began to laugh. "That is the one you brought in," He explained.

Maybe our lives aren't as bad as they seem.

A Change of Jobs

Mr. Wilson needed to get to a business meeting from the airport. He caught a taxi in the large city and gave the taxi driver the address of his meeting.

A few minutes later, he thought he would ask the taxi driver how long it would take to get to their destination. He tapped the taxi driver on the shoulder so he could ask the question.

The taxi driver jumped, almost went to the other side of the road, and almost hit the median before he came to a stop.

"I did not mean to startle you," Mr. Wilson said, a little shaken up.

"Oh," the taxi driver replied, "it's not your fault. You see, this is my first day on the job after driving corpses to the cemeteries for years," he explained.

What Is It?

━━━ ⚖ ━━━

My tiny dog loves to lie and sleep on the couch, where he can watch all the activities in our fenced backyard. This morning, he jumped up and started barking and running to the door. There was a blue plastic sack blowing all over the yard in the wind.

It's Not What You Think

During the COVID shutdown, there was a picture of three policemen guarding the toilet-paper section in a grocery store. There was also a video of a shady character walking down the road carrying a large sack over his shoulder. He was looking in every direction to be sure no one was watching him.

A car pulled up beside him. "How much do you have?" the guy asked the person in the car while looking in every direction.

The person pulled out a roll of bills. The shady person grabbed the roll of bills while still looking in every direction. "This will do," he said and pulled out a roll of toilet paper. He also handed the other person a bottle of disinfectant at no charge before he hurried on.

Bible: What is the most important thing in your world?

Get Organized

━┿━ ⊨◆⊨ ━┿━

Two men were walking down the street together. They were rather large men and had muscles bulging from their arms below their short sleeves. They passed a doorway where two other strong men were trying to carry a baby grand piano.

"Would you like some help?" one of the men on the street asked.

"That would be nice," one of the men in the doorway answered.

The four men tried and tried but could not move the piano.

"I guess we will just have to leave it until we get even more help," the doorway man said.

"Oh, you were coming out with it. We thought you were going in with it," the street man said.

Bible: Things are better when we all work together.

Gotcha

I was about eight years old when my grandparents on my daddy's side decided to spend the day with us. It was April 1 and April Fool's Day. I had spent most of the day picking on my grandpa and telling him things that were not true. When he would look, I would shout, "April Fool's Day!" I guess it was a day one could get by not telling the truth.

Grandpa had been a good sport and laughed along with me.

Our dining-room table was in front of two large windows. I was sitting on the side that was facing away from the windows.

We were eating and laughing when my grandpa stopped talking and looked my way with his mouth dropped open. Everyone else was looking that way too. Grandpa said very slowly, "Jeanie, there is a bear looking at you through the window."

Without looking, I screamed and ran over to the other side of the table next to my mother.

Everyone started laughing when Grandpa said, "April Fool's Day."

Even to this day, seventy-five years later, I can still see a large bear looking through that large window at me. Grandpa got even.

Up until that time, no one had sighted a bear in our area of the High Plains in southern Colorado. When I was a teenager, I remember this story about an area about thirty miles west of us.

It seems that a small child came running in from playing outside. She was screaming, "Mommy, Mommy, there is a cow in our tree!"

The mother laughed and tried to explain to her that it was impossible that a cow could be in a tree.

The child persisted until the mother went out to check. Sure enough, there was a large bear in their tree. The rangers had to capture it and take it out west to where it was supposed to be.

That reminds me of the time my husband and I were running a large number of cattle on the national grasslands near our farm. It was the time of the year that the calves were born. We noticed that some of the cows would graze while the other cows would stand close to where the calves were lying, forming a circle.

We thought this was peculiar.

One day, I was out counting the cattle when I had to go through a gate in the fence. Sand had blown onto the road going through the gate. When I was latching the gate, I looked down. I saw cat tracks that were huge. You could tell that the cat had jumped over the gate, and the tracks were where it had landed in the sand.

Then we knew the cows were trying to protect their babies from a mountain lion that had wandered into our area from the mountains. We didn't lose any cattle or calves.

Bible: God gave man the power over all the animals.

Mind Your Mama

<figure>━━ ⬥ ━━</figure>

I had a cousin who was almost two years older than me. Because of family circumstances, she spent her summers when she wasn't in school with my family on our farm. It was in the 1940s, from the time I was ten to thirteen.

We had a lot of fun together, but we got into trouble when we didn't mind my parents. I'm sure we were good most of the time, but those times weren't as memorable as the times we were not so good.

It was harvesttime. Late one night, I said to my cousin, "Daddy is just coming down the road to the house with a truckload of grain. Let's sneak out and scare him when he gets out of the truck."

As usual, Mandy said okay with a giggle.

It was pretty dark when we slipped out of the house and quietly snuck up on the other side of the truck. We waited for Daddy to turn around after checking the canvas and bungee cords over the grain.

Just as Daddy turned around to walk into the house, he made a terribly loud noise, raising his large hands toward us.

The noise startled and scared us so much that we ran into each other while running back into the house. I think I heard my father laughing.

Mandy and I discovered it was fun to jump off the outside toilet.

"You girls quit jumping off the toilet right now! You might get hurt!" Mother shouted from the back door of our house. She turned around and went back inside.

"This is so much fun. Let's do it one more time," I said.

Just as I jumped, Mandy said something funny. I laughed just as I landed on the ground. My chin hit my knee, and I bit a hole through my tongue. I was bleeding badly as we had to go to the house, and we knew we were in trouble. Mandy was crying as hard as I was.

"Mother, Mandy and I want to make a playhouse in the brooder house since the chickens are large enough to brood in the hen house. We can clean it up and save you some work," I said.

"I think you can have fun in there, but you can't clean it up until I have time to help you," Mother answered. "Don't start on it until I can help you. Do you understand?" she said again.

Mother was extra busy that day, and we girls were tired of waiting.

"Maybe if we sneak out there and clean up the brooder house and surprise her so she won't have to do it, it just might be a good thing to do," I suggested.

We grabbed a couple of brooms, a duster, and a mop and bucket and went to the brooder house when we thought she wasn't looking. It was fun to remove all the debris from the little building and to plan where we were going to put our play furniture. When we finished, we felt itchy and were not feeling well, so we went to the house to rest.

Mandy was leaning on the ironing board where Mother was ironing a black dress. Mother stopped several times to brush "dust" from the black dress. All of a sudden, she screamed, "Those white spots are moving! You girls disobeyed me and have been in the brooder house, and now you are covered with chicken mites!" she screamed again. "I will have to wash you in coil oil and wash your clothes," she said, very disappointed.

The itching and smell were punishment enough at that time.

There was one time we did better.

People used to buy flour in printed cotton sacks. Mother saved the sacks and made clothes out of them. One year, she made Mandy and me beautiful dresses out of flour sacks. The dresses were just alike.

"Would you girls like to wear your new dresses and ride the bus from here to Lamar? It is time for Mandy to go home and get ready for another school year," Mother said. "I can pick you up at the bus station and take you to Mandy's house," she explained.

We felt so grown up to ride the bus for fifty miles all by ourselves, and we acted like adults. What fun!

After Mandy and I became adults, we talked and discovered something we did know as kids. Mandy was jealous of me because I had a good father, and I was jealous of Mandy because she was prettier than me. She had a nice color and black hair like I had always wanted since I had red hair, white skin, and freckles.

Song: Precious memories, how they linger.

Miracles

Encounter with Angels?

I have had several encounters that can't be explained. Maybe if we were not so brainwashed, we could see more of God's power.

A young man just out of high school was racing a friend in their new vehicles. His mother had a vision two weeks before when she saw her son hit something in the middle of the road. She could not see what he hit, but the car was totaled. In her vision, she saw six angels take the hood of the car and carry her son away from the accident. She asked her husband to pray with her that her son was all right.

Two weeks later, her son was racing with another car one night when it hit a cow in the middle of the highway. The state trooper estimated that her son's car was going about 120 miles an hour. He was thrown a great distance from the car but sustained no injuries. The front of the car was completely gone.

The young man said when he was flying through the air, there was a blue light around him, and he knew he would be all right.

The mother knew he would be all right but cried with thanksgiving when she saw what was left of the vehicle.

In another vision, the mother had been called over to the hospital to identify her son's body. She woke up crying and said to her husband, "Wake up and pray with me. My son is in trouble again."

The couple prayed. They learned later that at the very time they were praying, the son was coming home alone from a rock concert in the capital city when he went to sleep. Something shook him and woke him up just before he hit a cement culvert in the middle of the highway. God answers prayer.

Who Was There?

The Thomas family had just lost their farm in a bank foreclosure. George had found a job working for a health-foods company to make some income. He had to travel to different places, setting up and conducting meetings for the new company. Alice could not travel with him until she finished her teaching job for the summer.

It was a time of a lot of difficulties. They were still living on the family farm. Winter was almost over, but it was very cold, and the water pipes were frozen.

There were some strange stories about the farm when George's parents had lived there. It was the first time Alice had been on the farm alone. She had decided not to be afraid as she climbed into the large lounge chair next to the large bed in the master's bedroom with a good book. The red velvet drapes and bedspread made the room feel warm.

Alice had just read a few pages when she realized that she was waking up. "If I am this sleepy, I guess I will get ready for bed and can just 'fall in' the next time I feel myself going to sleep," she told herself.

As Alice walked into the kitchen and turned on the stove to warm up some water and brush her teeth, she realized that the two large dogs were barking at something outside. "Here I am alone and twelve miles from town. I guess I better turn off all the lights, so whoever it is will think there is no one at home," she thought as she quickly turned off three lights.

Alice ran to the kitchen window and looked through the curtain at the front door. There was a man standing there. About that time, she heard not a knock but a voice that sounded like *ma* and saw a hand sliding down the door. Alice ran back to the kitchen window and looked at the front porch again.

This time, the person at the front door turned around, and his large flashlight lit up his face. It looked like Alice's father.

"Mother must be sick," Alice whispered as she ran toward the door. Then she quickly stopped. "It can't be Daddy because he went to heaven two years ago!" Alice exclaimed. She ran back to the kitchen window and looked again. There was no one there, but she saw the backlights of a Buick pulling out of the driveway. Her father had always driven Buicks.

Alice went back to the bedroom and dialed a friend in town. When Vera Lee answered, she told her what had just happened.

"I just wanted to call you and see if I am really awake or not," she explained.

"Alice, you need to come to town and spend the night with me. I think it is dangerous for you to be out there alone," Vera Lee said.

"I'm not frightened, and I think I will just stay inside," Alice said. "It was probably someone needing help, and I was not brave enough to answer the door and help," she added.

The next few days, Alice asked her sons and the neighbors if they had come by. Everyone said no. She could not forget the incident where someone had needed help, and she didn't help.

That summer, Alice was able to travel with George on his business trips. On one of these trips, she saw a vision of what happened that night on the farm. She had been in more danger than she realized. The dogs were barking at something she could not see, and the "person" who was at the door was there to get rid of her. She saw that when he tried to knock on the door, the house was covered with the blood of Jesus, and he lost all his power and left.

The only thing Alice could relate the incident to was an event that had taken place months before. Alice and George had been attending a new church in town that was still meeting in people's homes. An elderly man came to one of these meetings. He was one of the leaders of a group who thought they talked to dead spirits.

The minister had asked if anyone needed healing. The man walked up to the minister and said, "I do."

The minister said, "I know who you are and how you believe. I want you to know that you have to believe in Jesus because He is the one who heals."

The man replied, "My wife told me not to come here. We have to believe the way we do because we even have videos of the dead people we talk to."

The man wanted to say more, but the minister asked him to leave. He did not want the young people there to hear ungodly stories.

As the man stomped out of the house, Alice felt sorry for him and asked the minister if he had any scriptures she could share with the man. The minister gave her two scriptures, and she and George followed the man out to his vehicle. He was carrying a Bible.

"Wait. I want to share these scriptures with you before you leave," Alice said.

The man looked at the scriptures and said, "I thought I believed in this book, but I don't guess I do." He threw the Bible into the backseat. Then he turned to look at George and Alice. "I have been pretty sick, and I know if you people pray for me, I can be well."

"As the minister said, healing only comes from Jesus," George tried to explain.

"I am a wealthy man, and I would not miss forty thousand dollars," the man said.

"We can't take your money. God does not charge for healing," Alice tried to explain.

"Well, you are good kids, and you believe the way you do, and I will be satisfied to believe like I do," the old man said.

"That is not true," Alice said. "If you are satisfied in the way you believe, then what are you doing here tonight?" she asked.

The old man started the car, made a quick U-turn in his vehicle, and sped off at high speed, throwing dust on Alice and George. Might there be a connection to what happened to Alice that night on the farm?

Not the Ending of Life but the Beginning

My late husband loved the Lord and did not want anyone to miss heaven. We had traveled to the city to visit some of my relatives. My aunt was in a nursing home. She was very sick and screamed a lot. The family decided it was too sad to visit her.

My husband and I were determined to see her. Maybe for the last time. We drove to the nursing home and could hear her screams when we climbed out of our car in the parking lot.

"Help me, help me! Please, will someone help me!" Auntie screamed.

It was hard to go in. When we entered the room, we could not tell if she recognized us or not. And her body was so swollen we did not recognize her. She was still screaming, "Help me!"

John put his arms around Aunt Mable and started talking to her. "God loves us, and He wants to help us," he said several times. Then John prayed over her.

Aunt Mable stopped screaming. I happened to have my keyboard, and we sang a few church songs for her. We prayed with her and got ready to leave. It was quiet when we crawled back into our car.

Aunt Mable moved to heaven that night.

We were visiting another aunt in a nursing home, Aunt Ellen. We tried to drive to the city and visit her every month. We would have a good visit and sing some church songs with my keyboard and pray before we left.

One time, we had just finished praying when we opened our eyes. There was a beautiful nurse wearing a white uniform standing by the closet. She had olive skin and long black hair.

"Has your aunt ever accepted Jesus as her Lord and Savior?" the nurse asked.

"I think so," I answered.

"I'm worried about her," the nurse replied.

"Aunt Ellen, have you ever accepted Jesus as your Lord and Savior?" I asked.

"Not that I remember," Aunt Ellen answered.

"Would you like to do that now?" I asked.

"Yes, I believe I would," Aunt Ellen answered.

John led Aunt Ellen in prayer, and Aunt Ellen repeated his words.

When we opened our eyes, the beautiful nurse was gone. We asked everyone at the home, and no one had seen anyone with that description.

That was the last time we saw Aunt Ellen because she moved to heaven before our next trip to the city. But we shall see her again someday, and we believed later that the nurse was an angel.

My youngest aunt was mentally challenged. She never learned to read or write. But she was a believer in God. One time, when she was staying with us, another aunt and her daughter were in a car accident, and both ended up in the hospital. My mother was concerned and exclaimed, "What are we going to do?"

My aunt quickly answered, "Pray, kiddo, pray!"

When my aunt moved to heaven, the family gave me her Bible. I still have it. It has a lot of scriptures underlined and side notes in her own special language besides some scriptures.

She was happy when a lot of her brothers and sisters were not because she knew the Lord.

What Happened in the Bible Can Still Happen Today

It was back in the 1980s. My husband and I were farming in the panhandle of Oklahoma. Jim was using road-grading equipment to level out more land to make it suitable for farming. There were a lot of sand dunes, tumbleweeds, and soap weeds on the land.

We left the field and drove home late one evening. As we were getting ready to eat supper, Jim said, "I was really frightened today."

"About what?" I asked as I put the sandwiches on the table.

"I dug up a den of rattlesnakes under some soap weeds. They scattered everywhere, and one of them chased me back on the tractor," Jim explained.

"Wow," I said with a shiver going down my spine. I tried to forget about it when we went back to work in the fields the next morning.

The next week, I was planting wheat on the "new" land. There was still a lot of debris on the land, and I had to stop often to clean the trash out of the planter shanks. I would sit on the ground and reach as far above the shank as I could and pull the dried weeds from the shank. I had just crawled back into the tractor and started down the field when my left arm, right above my wrist, began to hurt. "I must have poked my arm with some dried tumbleweeds," I told myself.

My arm was hurting worse, and I felt it throbbing. I stopped the tractor and pulled up my sleeve to see my injury. Just above my left wrist were two puncture marks about two inches apart. My arm was terribly swollen and turning black. I knew what had happened.

I was in the field alone. It was thirty miles to the nearest doctor. It was a helpless situation.

"Oh Lord, it says in the Bible that the apostle Paul was bitten by a poisonous viper, and it did not hurt him. He just shook it off and went about his work. I am claiming the same thing for my arm," I said and kept planting the wheat. My arms stopped hurting, and when I crawled off the tractor that evening, the swelling was gone.

I was so thankful and excited about telling my husband about it. When I told him the story, the puncture marks were even gone, and he didn't believe my story. I still know that my loving Heavenly Father saved my life that day, and I still thank him when I remember it.

When Mount St. Helens erupted 1,500 miles away in Washington, the air above that Oklahoma land had a purple glow in the evening from the ash that had traveled that far.

Angel Protection

We were living in Colorado Springs and working for a company that sold health products. My husband was putting ads in the paper about our products and when and where our meeting was going to be. We were trying to get others to join the company. Often, we had meetings in our homes.

One day, when I was home alone, I received a terrifying phone call. The caller said that he wanted to join our company. I said great, but my husband would have to help him with the papers. Then the caller said, "I like the way your breasts are shaped, and I am coming right over."

Shocked, I replied, "I'm just an old grandma, and you don't know where I live."

"Oh, I know where you live," the caller said. By this time, he was breathing deeply.

I was terrified and called my husband. Car phones had just become available, and he answered. I told him about the call.

"I think I know who it is. He was at our last meeting. One of our new distributors was showing the products. She was very nervous. The guy said the same thing about her breasts, but Betty was so nervous she didn't hear it, so I didn't say anything. I was glad he left quickly and didn't join," my husband explained.

"I am frightened," I said.

"Oh, I don't think you are in any danger, but I will come straight home," my husband replied.

I had a hard time sleeping that night. I could not get the phone call out of my mind.

My husband didn't think it was so funny when he showed me the newspaper the next morning. It reported a triple murder not far from where we lived. A single mother and her teenage son and teenage daughter had all been murdered. The two women had been sexually attacked. The mother's boyfriend had been questioned and released.

The newspapers reported the story for several days, but the murderer had not been found. I finally called the police and asked for the person who was in charge of the Valentine Murders. I told him about my phone call.

"I am sorry you had an ugly phone call, but it has nothing to do with this case," the man said.

"But I could tell that the man on the phone had needs that he was going to fill no matter what," I replied.

"Sorry, but it has nothing to do with my case," he said and hung up.

The murderer was never found.

I still praise God for his protection during that time.

Protection in a Foreign Land

Back in the '50s and '60s, the nation of Buremby, Africa, was in a civil war. The government had taken over and tried to kill all Christians and anyone who could read and write. They were also killing all the tall people of a certain tribe.

The missionaries who were serving in this area had sent their children to a Christian school some distance away. The government army marched toward the school, planning to kill everyone. The students and teachers prayed for God's protection and waited. They heard the chanting of the oncoming army, but no one came into the complex.

School started the next morning, the same as usual. It was still quiet. No one knew what had happened until some of the government army men were talking to the people in the village.

"We don't know what happened last night, but when we tried to destroy that school, we kept running into a wall. We could not see the wall, but it was there, and several men were injured trying to go through it. It was really scary, and we finally gave up and left," one man said.

Everyone praised the Lord for protecting their children, teachers, and other people who were in the complex.

Later, the missionaries had to leave the country, but the native Christians were finally able to keep the churches going.

On the Highway

Tim and Jane were traveling on Highway I-80 from South Dakota. They had just finished visiting Tim's relatives. Jane took her keyboard from the backseat, and they were singing church songs when Jane realized Tim was not singing. He was going eighty miles an hour and slumped down in his seat.

Tim was a tall man, and Jane had a hard time taking over the steering wheel and getting Tim's large foot off the pedal. She was finally able to bring the car to a stop, and Tim crawled out.

"What are you doing?" Tim asked. He sounded and acted drunk, but Tim did not drink.

"You almost wrecked us!" Jane exclaimed.

"So what?" Tim said with a giggle.

With some coaxing, Jane was able to get Tim into the passenger side of the car. She pulled out on the highway, wanting to stop a state trooper for help. They met a patrol car going the other way, but it turned around and pulled in behind them as Jane pulled off the road.

"Something is wrong with my friend, and I don't know where any medical facilities are around here!" Jane exclaimed.

The trooper looked at Tim and nodded. "There is a small town about five miles from here. The doctor's office is next to the hospital. Follow me," he said. The officer quickly led them to the town.

A nurse came out and checked Tim, and they soon had him loaded into the town ambulance. Jane had a hard time keeping up as she followed the ambulance to Pierre. By the time Jane parked the car, Tim was in a hospital room. She called some of Tim's children to let them know where they were and that their father was sick.

Jane was concerned as she waited in the waiting room. Finally, a pretty nurse came out of Tim's room and walked down the hall. She sat down beside Jane. "Tim is going to be all right. I am his sister," she said.

Jane could hardly believe that this was one relative she had not met at the family dinners.

In a short time, Tim was dismissed, and they went to Sister Ellen's house to rest. By the time some of Tim's family arrived, he seemed to be as good as usual. They were glad that Jane had called them and had another good visit while they were still in South Dakota.

Tim moved to heaven in his sleep two weeks later.

Thank you, Lord, for protecting us on the highway.

Several years later, Jane remarried. Jane retired from teaching in 1990. Bob retired a few years later. He worked until he was sixty-nine. "It will be great to take a trip for once and not have to worry about coming home at a certain time and going back to work," Bob said. He and Jane were excited as they planned what they called their long trip.

Their easternmost destination was Minnesota to visit Jane's cousin, and they stopped in Kansas on the way to visit another cousin. In Minnesota, Cousin Dee showed them places of interest in his hometown, from a world-famous cereal factory to the very bank where the James gang did their last robbery eighty years earlier. They drove into Minneapolis and crossed over a bridge in the city. That bridge collapsed two weeks later.

Jane and Bob traveled to North Dakota to visit Bob's granddaughter and her family. Her children were two and four at the time.

It took a whole day to cross Montana. Their next destination was to visit Jane's uncle in western Washington. They had a great visit with another aged uncle in Yakima on the way. The next morning, they crossed Washington to the ocean side of the state where Jane's other uncle and family lived on Whidbey Island.

"Let's stop here on this side of Deception Pass Bridge and take some pictures," Jane said.

The green forest and ocean were great backgrounds for the pictures. They crossed over the high bridge connecting the island to the mainland. Two miles down the island road, Bob pulled off the highway.

"What are you stopping here for?" Jane asked.

"I am too dizzy to drive anymore," Bob answered and started vomiting.

Jane was not used to driving in different places, but she had no choice. She was shaking as she tried to help Bob and drive through traffic. She parked in an alley behind a grocery store in the small town.

Bob was very sick. When he was able to sit up, Jane tried to find the road that led to her uncle's home. She was looking for Phoenix Road instead of Scenic Road. She had to call her aunt twice to get the right name.

Jane's aunt and cousin came out of the house to help her get Bob into the house. He had lost all sense of direction and was running into things.

Bob thought he was having a bad reaction from some cold medicine he had taken. He became even sicker, and at midnight, Jane called the hospital. Bob was picked up by the ambulance. The young doctor at the hospital told Bob if he could walk to the bathroom and back, he could go home.

Relatives helped Bob into the house again. He grew so much worse that Jane had to call for the ambulance again. This time, they decided that Bob had had a cardiac attack and stroke. They did not know if he was going to make it or not. A week later, he was sent to a rehabilitation hospital two hundred miles north. A cousin drove them there.

"Thank you, Lord, for getting us across the high bridge before Bob almost died," Jane has said many times.

More Road Protection

It was dark, and Jane was driving home from town. The dirt road had just been road graded, and the wind was blowing.

Suddenly Jane saw some creature in the middle of the road. She thought it was a skunk when the eyes of the animal reflected the car light close to the ground. Then she saw a large outline. A large black cow was in front of her, and she didn't have time to stop. She turned the car to where the animal would hit the highest part of the front bumper.

The cow died, and Jane had a large bump on her forehead where she had hit the windshield, but the pink Cadillac was totaled.

"Thank you, Lord, for protecting me," Jane said.

God will put His angels in charge over you. They will lift you up with their hands lest you dash your foot against a stone.

Protection at Home

Betty had only been home two months after spending two months in a hospital in the state capital. She was recovering from a brain infection and was learning how to do many simple things all over again. Her husband was working long hours on the family farm twenty-five miles away.

Betty was working in the yard when she realized she was locked outside of the house. She had her telephone but did not have any telephone numbers with her. Betty couldn't remember any number. It would be at least five hours before her husband was to come home from the field.

Betty sat down in one of the lawn chairs to try to wait when she heard a familiar sound. It was her husband's truck coming down the road four hours early.

"I am so glad to see you," Betty said. "What made you come home early?" she asked.

"I could not get you off my mind, so I thought I needed to come home and see if you were okay," he answered.

"Thank you, Lord," Betty said with a sigh.

Never Forget

My stepfather had played the guitar most of his life. When he became a part of our family after my father died, he was a Gideon. When he had a speaking engagement at a church, he would play the guitar and sing. As he grew older, he had dementia and went several years not playing the guitar or singing.

One holiday, our family was together at my son's home. My son had just finished playing the guitar for us when my daughter-in-law took the guitar and put it in my stepdad's hands. My stepdad began to play like he had never stopped.

The family listened and clapped. My daughter-in-law said, "Wayne, you did a great job of playing the guitar."

"No, I didn't play the guitar," my stepfather said.

"Yes, you did," she said.

After some arguing, my daughter said, "You did play the guitar, and I took a video of it and can prove it."

Wayne watched the video and said, "I guess I did, didn't I?"

Healing Power

One afternoon, Raul promised a friend that he would go down into the car pit in his neighbor's garage and see what trouble she was having with her car. He was a good mechanic and thought he could help his friend. He did not know he was standing in gas. Before he knew it, a spark lit the gas, and he was caught in flames. Raul ran but before the flames could be put out, he was burned over 60 percent of his body.

Raul was flown to the burn center in the state capital. He prayed and felt very little pain. The doctors thought he would lose his eyesight and experience other concerns. There were many skin grafts. One surgery developed an infection, and Raul lost three fingers. His eyes gradually healed. Raul knew it was an attack from the enemy.

Raul just put his life in Jesus's hands. He decided that since the devil had put him in this predicament, he would make it count. When he was able to walk with a walker, he went around talking to people in the hospital about the good news of the gospel.

Many times, he would start by asking people if they were happy. Most of them were not. Then he would say, "Look at me. I am joyful and happy because I know Jesus as my Savior." He was able to pray the prayer of salvation with many people, both medical and people healing from terrible burns.

Raul is now at home with his family and active in his church. He is still sharing his faith with others.

More Protection on the Road

A cousin of mine was traveling with his family one night to a small town when the car began to shake and lose power. He was not a mechanic and had no idea what the trouble might be. Bob stopped the car and did not know what to do when another car pulled off the road behind them. A man crawled out of the car and came to the window.

"It looks like you are having car trouble. Would you mind opening the hood so I can look at it?" the man said.

"I sure would appreciate it because I'm not a mechanic," Bob said.

The man looked under the hood and quickly said, "You are having filter trouble. I just happen to have a filter as you need in the trunk of my car. Would you mind if I put it in?" he asked.

"Sure," Bob said with a sigh.

The man put in the new filter, and the car ran smoothly.

"Thanks a lot!" Bob said, but the man was no longer there. "Thank you, Lord!" Bob said. "I guess I have to believe in angels now."

School Funnies

Years ago, I was getting ready to start the school day with my sixth graders when Michelle held up her hand.

"Yes, Michelle," I said.

"I just wanted to tell you that my brother ran into the drugstore last night."

"So?" I responded.

"Well, he tore up the front of the store pretty bad and broke the large window in front," Michelle explained.

I could hear the kids laughing.

Another Road Story

There is a small town in Kansas where two very tall elevators were built too close to the road. A sign warns travelers to be aware of the dangerous winds that are possible on that part of the highway.

The Wilson family had borrowed a car from some friends to make the journey from another state to a town on the other side of the elevators.

No one knows for sure what happened, but they guess that a whirlwind had gained strength going past the elevators. The first thing they knew was that the car was carried by the winds, crashing it into the side of one of the buildings. The car was badly damaged and caught on fire.

The Wilsons were unable to open the doors when a man in a bright-blue suit showed up and forced the doors open. He helped each family member out of the car and far away to safety before the car exploded.

The Wilson family was so thankful for his help, but when they turned to thank him, he was not there. They looked in every direction but could not see anyone. They are sure it was an angel. No one was badly injured.

Protection in College

Jane was taking fifteen graduate hours at the university. She and her husband were poor, and Jane was hoping the grain check from her father's estate would be enough money to pay the expenses.

One of Jane's classes was located on the third floor of one of the buildings. One night Jane had to stay after class to ask her professor some questions.

The building was deserted as Jane descended the steps. She was thinking about the woman who had been murdered the week before over by the engineering building. The murderer had not been caught.

When Jane stepped outside, she realized it was so foggy that she could barely see her hand in front of her face. This did not make her feel any safer. As Jane inched her way toward the parking lot where she had left her truck, she heard a man's footsteps behind her. She was so frightened that she turned around in hopes of seeing who was following her.

A handsome tall man with large muscles came into view. Jane held back a scream when she heard the man say," It is awfully spooky around here tonight. Can I walk with you to the parking lot?" he asked.

"Who would attack someone like you?" Jane whispered to herself. "I guess it would be all right," she answered.

When they reached the parking lot, the fog had lifted enough that Jane could see her truck. "Thank you for walking with me," Jane said, but there was no one there. "It must have been an angel protecting me from harm," Jane told herself.

It was the last day of class, and the grain check had not come in. Jane was very upset when there was no mail in their post-office box.

"I have worked so hard the last four months and even did a lot of hours in fieldwork for one class and borrowed money from my mother for my books, and I am going to lose it all," Jane sighed. "Oh Lord, help me, please!" she prayed. Just then, she heard someone calling her name.

"Mrs. Jones, I think this should have been put in your box," the lady said, handing Jane an envelope.

The letter was from the grain company. Jane quickly opened the envelope. The amount of the check was fifty dollars more than her tuition. She had thirty minutes to get to the bank, cash the check, and get to the university before the office closed.

Jane drove as fast as she could to the bank and then to the university, but by the time she had climbed the three flights of stairs and run down the hall, the office, with the bars on the windows, was closed. She started pounding on the door. Eventually, a lady opened the door.

"I need to pay my tuition," Jane shouted. "Can you take it this late?" she asked.

"I guess we will," the lady replied. "You should be more responsible and not pay your debts at the last minute," she said gruffly.

"If you only knew how much I would like to," Jane said to herself. "Thank you, Lord!" Jane said as she floated down the stairs. It seemed impossible that the world was so much brighter than it was a few minutes ago.

Jane stopped on her way home to put ten dollars of gas in her truck. She gave the man her fifty-dollar bill, and he handed her a ten-dollar bill back.

"I gave you a fifty-dollar bill," Jane said.

"No, you didn't," the attendant argued.

"I know I gave you a fifty because that is all I had!" Jane shouted.

"Look in my drawer and see that there is no fifty-dollar bill there!" the attendant shouted back.

Jane lost the argument and was not able to buy as many groceries as she was planning to, but the Lord always took care of them, no matter what.

Supplies on the Mountain

I would like to share a story a friend told me—again. She was the mother of one of my high school students:

> I was in a terrible marriage and was putting up with a lot from my husband. One night, he came home with another woman and wanted to do some very strange things. I knew our family was not safe with him anymore, so I left him and took my daughter and two sons and moved into a small cabin on the side of a mountain.
>
> It was winter and there was about two feet of snow on the mountain. We had not received any money from the government and ran out of food and wood for the stove and fireplace. Like the widow in the Bible, I fed my kids our last meal, and we prayed before we went to bed.
>
> In the middle of the night, someone was knocking at the door. I opened the door and saw three large men standing by a sled. The sled was piled high with firewood.
>
> "We thought you might be needing some wood," one man said. "Where do you want us to put it?" he asked.
>
> "Oh, thank you," my friend replied. "Just put it against the south side of the cabin," she suggested.
>
> "Would you mind if we bring in some of it and put it next to the fireplace?" the man asked.

"That would be great if you don't mind," the mother replied.

When she stepped outside to thank the men again, there was no one there. "I wonder how they pulled the sled away so quickly," she wondered.

Just as it turned to daylight, there was another knock on the cabin door. My friend said when she opened the door this time, there were two large men beside a sled. The sled was loaded with groceries. The two men brought in the groceries and seemed to disappear as quickly as the first sled had done.

The family went to town that day and tried to find out which church, or churches, had brought their survival supplies. They could never find anyone who knew anything about the wood or food.

My friend said the supplies lasted the rest of the winter until they moved off the mountain and she could find a job. "I have thanked the Lord many times for saving us from starvation and freezing to death," she said.

Masks

The year 2020 was interesting, and because of the COVID epidemic, everyone was wearing masks. One day at work, our supervisor needed to go to Walmart for some supplies.

She came back laughing. She said, "I saw this lady in the store, and her hair looked just like a friend of mine. I guess she thought she knew me too, and after we hugged, we removed our masks and realized we did not know each other."

Another friend said, "I just read in the paper that a woman came home from her shopping, and the man she had just brought home with her removed his mask, and it was not her husband."

We had visitors one day at our business. One was slender and had beautiful long black hair. I could not tell if it was a man or a woman. I was shocked when he took off his mask, and he had a full thick beard underneath.

Who could ever imagine that the whole world would look like bank robbers and the toilet section in the stores would be guarded by the police? I never did learn how to eat, drink, or lick stamps while wearing a mask.

Bob and Joyce

In the past, they were called mentally retarded. Today they are called special people, and that was just what Bob and Joyce were.

Jim went to the same church as my cousin. While I was going through my second divorce, my cousin wrote me:

> I know you must have a dim view of men. Not all men are bad. Jim is a guy who goes to my church. His wife died five years ago from cancer. He is a nice guy and active in our church, and I know he is lonesome. I thought you might like to write to each other. His address is Fourth Street, Holdrege, Nebraska.

Jim and I were pen pals for some time before we ever met and eventually ended up getting married. He had to work

Saturdays, so I drove the 220 miles every weekend and stayed with my cousin so we could date.

The first summer after we married, I lived in Nebraska with Jim and went to his church. He played baseball and basketball on the church team, drove the church bus to take children to church, and used his own vehicle to pick up Bob and Joyce from two different group homes.

Bob and Joyce were in their forties. Bob was tall and slender, walked like a horse galloping, and had trouble talking so people could understand him.

Joyce was blind, short, and plump. She had trouble talking and was bald. She wore a wig and always looked neat. She always wanted me to hold her hand when we were around other people.

Jim and I were eventually able to understand them when they talked.

One Sunday morning, Jim picked me up, and then we drove across town to pick up Joyce so she could sit with me in the backseat. Next, we picked up Bob. Bob was wearing a new shirt and pants. The pants were about two sizes too large for his slender figure. Jim helped him pull them up a couple of times while walking to the car and more times while walking into the church.

We had a retired minister guest speaker that morning. He preached a simple message on salvation and then invited anyone who wanted to open their lives to Jesus and accept His salvation to hold up their hand. Then the speaker invited people to come forward to pray.

I opened my eyes to see if Bob and Joyce were okay. I was pleasantly surprised to see Bob holding up his hand. He looked very serious. Since he had a hard time walking and talking, I didn't know what to do.

The minister prayed with the people who had come forward and prayed a final prayer and dismissed the congregation. He quickly walked over to where we were standing. He asked Bob if he would like to accept Jesus as his savior. It was then he realized that Bob was a "special person." Bob was still determined and said a loud yes.

Gently, the old minister led Bob in a sinner's prayer, and Bob repeated the words as clearly as I had even heard him speak. I had never heard a more sincere prayer of asking Jesus to forgive them of their sins and come into their life.

Jim and I hugged our new "brother in Christ" as we laughed and cried. Joyce knew something exciting was going on and started jumping up and down and pulled off her wig. She looked like a bald-headed large baby.

Bob was happy and knew what had happened.

Jim went out to get the car and pick us up in front of the church. The large entrance was crowded with people leaving to go home.

Bob was still happy and excited as he "loped" out of the building ahead of Joyce and me. He suddenly realized he could not see Jim or me, and he panicked.

When Joyce and I came out of the church, Bob had lost his pants again. They were in a heap at his feet. He saw me and crawled over to me with his pants dragging on his feet. Bob grabbed me by the leg like a scared six-foot child.

Jim was soon there and helped me pull up Bob's pants and get a frightened man into the car and put Joyce's wig back on. We took the two special people back to their group homes. They were not only special but also precious.

Joyce was sick once. She was so glad when Jim and I went to the hospital to visit her. She recognized our voices and gave us big hugs.

Jim's company closed, and he moved to Colorado with me. We lost contact with Bob and Joyce. We don't know whether they are still living or not, but we are certain when we get to heaven, we will see two of God's special people there with hugs.

My father was the third child in a family of thirteen children. Aunt Margie was the youngest, and she was also a special person. She had gone to school for a short time but could not even learn to write her name.

Margie lived with my grandparents. After Grandpa died, Grandma could no longer take care of Margie and herself. She and Margie took turns living with my family and the family of one of my aunts. Eventually, Grandma was moved to a nursing home, and Margie was put into a group home.

While Aunt Margie was in the group home, she fell in love with one of the special guys at the home. She also had a lady friend at home, and the two ladies even did crafts together.

Both friends died a short time apart. Margie was heartbroken.

Margie finally ended up living with an older couple who thought of her as family. She eventually developed digestive problems but was not able to explain how she was feeling to anyone. The couple finally took her to the doctor, and she was quickly put in the hospital and on life support. Her brothers and sisters had to make the choice when she was taken off life support.

After my aunt's move to heaven, I was given her Bible. There were many scriptures underlined and many notes written beside the scriptures in her own language. She seemed to be happier than her brothers and sisters and wanted people to pray about things. I wonder if she was smarter than some of her family, but she was a loving special person.

"Oh Lord, I thank you for so many things. I love you so much, but how can I show it?" I prayed.

Then I heard deep inside me, "By showing my forgiveness and love to others."

Power

Mary was eighty-six years old. She had been a widow and tried to take care of her home. A friend introduced her to another friend who wanted to refinish Mary's old cabinets. He took a small door and refinished it, and it was very pretty. Mary did not know the man was an alcoholic and fell off the wagon when the work was to begin. Nine different people were sent to work on the cabinets that did not know what they were doing, so the cabinets were ruined. Stain and shiny finishing paints were everywhere, even some outside of the kitchen.

The Lord told Mary to keep a certain amount of money in her bank account for emergencies. Mary saved her money until

she thought she had enough to put in new cabinets. She called
two cabinet companies to try to order cabinets for her ruined
kitchen. They would not return her calls.

She waited and finally hired a contractor who was used to
remodeling old houses. He ordered the cabinets from a town two
hours away. His crew tore out the old cabinets and discovered
they didn't have enough cabinets to start the work. More had to
be ordered. Mary went four weeks without a kitchen. She used
a few dishes and washed them in the bathroom. She also had
Meals on Wheels delivered.

Mary had to keep her little dog on a leash to keep him out
of the workers' way. More cabinets had to be ordered, and the
deal was costing Mary three to four thousand dollars more than
she had planned. The last cabinet in the dining area was too
large, and another one had to be ordered. Then the contractor
took a two-week vacation. Mary had to pay to have the tile floor
repaired and the electrical wiring fixed, and she ended up having
to pay for their permits.

Mary was having trouble with a phosphate problem that
was causing her to be off balance. She had to keep herself from
falling. A friend had started walking a mile every day with her
and her dog when the friend's mother fell and broke her arm,
so her friend would be gone for six weeks, taking care of her
mother.

This morning, when Mary was getting ready to spend
her devotional time with the Lord, she heard herself laughing
uncontrollably. She was shouting at the devil. "Devil, I am
laughing at you. You thought you could take away my prosperity,
but I give my tithes and offerings, so you can't break me. I will
walk in love no matter what, and you can't take my health either

because Jesus not only died for my salvation but was also beaten for my health."

Mary remembered last month when she thought she had hurt her back and realized her back was hurting in the kidney area. "Back, I speak to you in the name of Jesus. Kidneys, in the name of Jesus, function the way you were created to function. I rebuke you, Satan, and get off my body in the name of Jesus." And her back had not hurt since that morning.

Praise God for His power, and we need to never forget it.

That Explains It

━━◆━━

Our country was going through a tough time. Many giveaway bills were being passed by our government for things we didn't need and things other countries didn't need. It will take generations of taxpayers to pay off the bills.

There was talk about making the people take shots against COVID. This came close to taking away our right to choose. People were living in fear, and many churches had been closed for a long time. There was little to laugh about until I heard a news commentator say, "The government people have taken shots to protect them from common sense."

"God can do anything except one thing. He has left the power of choice to humans. He can do anything but make a choice for people," I tried to explain.

Have you ever heard people say that God is not a good God or that the world would not be in this terrible mess? Or how could a good God send people to hell?

God has done everything He can do to show His love for us. Jesus, God's only Son, left heaven to come to this earth to teach us about the Father's love. He showed God's love by meeting people's needs, from healing to prosperity and even raising people from the dead. Jesus was beaten so that we could be healed, and He was murdered to pay the price for our sins so we don't have to. He took our place, and we have a way of forgiveness and an open door to heaven.

It is because of wrong choices that make our lives what they are and wrong choices that have messed up the world.

Jesus had to be born of a woman so He could take on an "earth suit" and defeat the devil legally since Adam gave up having authority over the earth to the devil. Jesus died and went to hell to defeat the devil for us. He showed him openly and took back the authority Adam had lost and gave it back to mankind when He rose from the dead. Then He went back to be at the right hand of the Father to make intercession for us and then sent the Holy Spirit to live in us and help us to make the right choices.

How can anyone doubt the love of God unless they just don't know what He has done? And how will they know unless someone tells them?

The Lord is *my* Shepherd (to *feed, guide,* and *shield* me). I *shall* not want. He *makes* me *lie* down in green pastures and *leads* me beside still waters. He *restores* my *soul*. He leads me in the paths of *rightness* with God, not for my earning it but for Jesus's sake.

Though I walk through the valley of death, I *will fear no evil* because you are with me. Your rod *to protect* and your staff *to guide*, they comfort me. You prepare a table for me in the presence of *my enemies*. You *anoint my head* with oil. My *brimming* cup runs over.

Surely, *mercy* and *goodness* shall follow me *all* the days of my life, and I shall *dwell* in the *house* of the Lord *forever*.

Which Is Better?

I was so glad when I learned from the Word of God that I am righteous because of what Jesus accomplished on the cross and not because of anything that I have done. He died for my past, present, and future mistakes; and now I can speak to Him boldly because of Jesus.

Now I can serve Him out of love and not fear of going to hell. It is so much easier and a whole lot more fun to serve Him this way. I don't think anyone has ever realized what a miracle this is. It was ever greater than the creation of the universe, which keeps growing, for Him to put his right standing with God on us. It was very expensive, but Jesus paid the price so he could have fellowship with us.

What more could He do besides being beaten for our healing and murdered for our salvation to show how much He loves us?

Visions

I was mourning over some military people who were killed by a suicide bomber. I heard the Lord say, "Look at it from My side." I saw the thirteen people coming into life beyond description. Every need was met, and they were extremely happy.

That helped me when I was mourning over a wreck where some teenagers were taken into God's presence a short time later.

Then I remembered a time when I had just lost my husband, and our family was having all kinds of problems. I cried out, "Lord, this is unfair. My family is having all these problems, and Jim is up there in heaven having a lot of fun."

I had just been around some people who thought only of themselves. They were unhappy and thought everyone was out to take advantage of them. It seemed that they were mad at the whole world. I had a vision where everyone had a huge rock in front of them that was blocking their view of everything. The rock had *me* painted on it. I watched while people were trying with all their might to get the rock out of the way so they could see.

Prayers

——— ✦ ———

Dear Heavenly Father, Daddy, I thank you for wanting fellowship, so you created the heaven and the earth and made man and put him in authority over the earth just so You could fellowship with him every day and subdue the earth together.

When man chose to fellowship with the devil instead, You had to send your laws to protect man from himself and others.

I thank you that you finally sent Your Son, Jesus, to this earth. I thank you, Jesus, that You were willing to be born of a woman to be able to take on an earth suit as we have. I thank you for growing up as we did but without sin and going about telling about the Father's love and showing the Father's love by meeting people's needs. Then You gave the ultimate sacrifice that through Your stripes, we are healed, and through Your blood, we are saved.

Thank you, Jesus, that You went to hell and defeated the devil and made a show of him openly. You took back the authority Adam lost and rose from the dead to give that authority back to mankind. Thank you for going back to heaven to make intercession for us at the right hand of the Father. Thank you for sending the Holy Spirit to us to be our advocate, comforter, and presence in times of trouble and to help us through this life so that we can spend eternity with you someday. In Jesus's name. Amen.

Dear Heavenly Father, I thank you for our school system. I thank you that we have teachers who believe in You. I thank you that our children and students are protected from wrong teaching, as well as violence and sickness. In Jesus's name. Amen.

Dear Heavenly Father, I thank you that Your people are taking part in politics by voting and running for any office when possible—that they will use their authority to stand up for Your laws and ideas and be open to Your knowledge, wisdom, and leadership. In Jesus's name. Amen.

Dear Heavenly Father, I thank you that my children are disciples taught by you, Lord, and great shall be the peace and undisturbed composure of my children. In Jesus's name. Amen.

Dear Heavenly Father, I thank you for that because I tithe my income and pay offerings, I am financially blessed, and all my needs are met. Nothing coming against me will prosper, and I can give to many, and I will never have to borrow. That I am the head and not the tail. I am not in bondage to anyone but walk in love toward my fellow man and with my God. In Jesus's name. Amen.

Dear Heavenly Father, I thank you that because Jesus was sacrificed, through His stripes, I am healed no matter how I feel.

Help me to believe your word above all that I see, feel, and hear. In Jesus's name. Amen.

What if you don't feel healed? Are you going to believe what the Word says or how you feel? Are you going to put God's healing words above everything else? What about when family and friends tell you that you are not healed?

We have to do like Jesus did when His very close friend John said he would not be going to the cross. "Get thee behind me, Satan, because you are saying the words of man and not of God."

Dear Heavenly Father, I thank you for loving me and going through each day with me with only good. Let me see Your blessings and miracles and joy throughout my day. In Jesus's name. Amen.

Inspired by Psalm 91

I dwell in the secret place of You, Most High, and remain stable and fixed under Your shadow, Almighty (whose power no one can withstand). I say to You, Lord, You are my refuge and my fortress, my God. In You, I lean and rely; and in You, I confidently trust!

For then, You will deliver me from the snare of the fowler and from the deadly pestilence. Then You will cover me with Your pinions, and under Your wings shall I trust and find refuge.

Your truth and Your faithfulness are a shield and a buckler. I shall not be afraid of the terror of the night or the arrow that flies by day or of the pestilence that stalks in darkness or of the destruction and sudden death that surprise and lay waste at noonday. Because I have made You, Lord, my refuge and You,

Most High, my dwelling place, there shall no evil befall me or any plague or calamity come near my home.

For You give Your angels charge over me to accompany, defend, and preserve me in all Your ways. They will bear me up with their hands lest I dash my foot against a stone. I shall treat upon the lion and adder. The young lion and the serpent I will put underfoot.

You set me on high because I know and understand Your name. (I have personal knowledge of Your love, mercy, and kindness, trusting and relying on You, knowing You will never forsake me—no, never. I shall call upon You, and You will answer me. You will be with me in trouble. You will deliver and honor me. With long life will You satisfy me and show me Your salvation. (As my days so shall my strength be.) Amen.

Inspired by Luke 11: 2–4

Our Father, Daddy, Daddy, who is in heaven, honored be Your name.

Your kingdom come, Your will be done on earth as it is in heaven. Give us this day our daily bread and forgive us our trespasses as we forgive those who trespass against us. Lead us not into temptation but deliver us from evil, for Yours is the kingdom, the power, and the glory forever. Amen.

Inspired by Psalm 23

You, Lord, are my shepherd to feed, guide, and shield me. I shall not want. You make me lie down in green pastures. You lead me beside the still waters. You refresh and restore my life.

You lead me in the paths of righteousness (right standing with God not for me earning it but for Jesus's sake). Though I walk through the deep and sunless valley of the shadow of death, I will fear no evil, for You are with me. Your rod to protect me and Your staff to guide me, they comfort me.

You prepare a table for me in the presence of my enemies. You anoint my head with oil; my brimming cup runs over. Surely, goodness and mercy will follow me all the days of my life; and through the length of my days, Your house and Your presence shall be my dwelling place. Amen.

Words of Inspiration

Back in the 1970s, there was a Western song that went like this: "You can't go roller skating in a buffalo herd, but you can be happy if you have a mind to."

I had thought about those words many times when things were not as I wanted them to be, like the following:

- Not having enough money to cover expenses
- Losing loved ones through death or divorce
- Caring for a sick child or other sick family members
- Going through a virus and pandemic
- Being afraid of many things, such as death, sickness, poverty, and darkness
- Going through loneliness

I had to choose to be happy anyway, which is impossible without God's help. To be joyful is the best way to defeat the devil.

The world is in bad shape because Christians (God's family) do not know the power they have or how to use it. Greater is He (the Holy Spirit) that is in us than he (the devil) that is in the world. God wants us to not only be conquerors but also more than conquerors. How do we know about this power and how to use it? By reading the manufacturer's manual: the Bible.

Praying in Tongues

Whether you believe in praying in tongues or not, think about this. God has given authority to mankind to speak words to accomplish things. It is up to man to speak words that have power if they agree with what His word says. When I pray about certain things, I usually don't know the circumstances to pray the right thing. That is when I start praying in tongues. God knows the circumstances, and I am praying His word.

For example, I prayed for a family member. I did not know that Kimberly and her husband were very sick, but God knew. That is why it is so important to pray in tongues.

I love You, Heavenly Father. I thank you that You wanted fellowship, so You created the heavens and the earth and made man and put him in authority over the earth so You could subdue the earth together and have fellowship every day. When Adam and Eve submitted to the devil, you had to send Your laws to protect many from themselves and others.

You finally sent Your only holy Son, Jesus, to this earth to help us.

Jesus, thank you for laying your deity in the hands of the Father and becoming a sperm in a woman so You could be born with an earth suit like we have and grow up like we did, except

You had no sin. Thank you for teaching us the Father's love and showing the Father's love by meeting people's needs through miracles.

Then You gave the ultimate sacrifice that through your stripes, we have been healed, and through Your blood, we have been saved and on our way to heaven.

Thank you that You went to hell so we won't have to and took back the authority man had lost, and then You rose from the dead to give that authority back to mankind. Then You went to heaven to make intercession for us at the right hand of the Father. And then You sent the precious Holy Spirit to live in us and help us. We are never alone and have a great guide through life.

Thank you, Holy Spirit, for being here and showing us how to use our authority and the power of Jesus's name in our daily lives.

I pray for the salvation of the leaders of governments across the world: China, Russia, North Korea, Mexico, Canada, South and Central Americas, Europe, and (Near East) Pakistan, Iran, Iraq, Afghanistan, and Palestine.

Are you feeling depressed? Try this. Make a list of one hundred things you are thankful for. Here are some in my list:

1) My salvation (I am on my road to heaven.)
2) My health (I go over healing scriptures every day.)
3) My prosperity (I have enough to meet my needs and enough to give to others.)
4) Prayer (The ruler of the universe gives me the privilege to talk with him.)
5) Love (God loves me even when I don't love myself.)

6) Family (I pray for them every day.)
7) Friends (I pray for them every day too.)
8) Food (I never go hungry.)
9) Furniture
10) Finances
11) Freedom
12) Water (RO, hot, cold, in-house, sprinkling system)
13) Bathrooms
14) Lights and electricity
15) Garage (My old car looks like new.)
16) My car
17) My security system, since I live alone
18) My computer so I can write my stories)
19) My watch
20) Stores close by, where I can buy everything I need
21) Police on the streets
22) Fire station in town
23) Good neighbors
24) My telephone and Facebook, texts, etc.
25) My hair, even though it is white now
26) My skin that holds me together
27) My trees that give me shade
28) The military that is protecting me
29) My little dog that keeps me company
30) Friends who come by
31) Friends who call
32) My clocks that change time automatically
33) The Bible, God's word speaking to me
34) My churches and encouragement
35) My church families and encouragement
36) My copier to make letters and cards
37) Add your own.

Printed in the United States
by Baker & Taylor Publisher Services